When the Nation Was in Need

Blacks in the Women's Army Corps During World War II

Martha S. Putney

The Scarecrow Press, Inc.
Lanham, Maryland, and London
2001

SCARECROW PRESS, INC.

Published in the United States of America
by Scarecrow Press, Inc.
4720 Boston Way, Lanham, Maryland 20706
www.scarecrowpress.com

4 Pleydell Gardens, Folkestone
Kent CT20 2DN, England

British Library Cataloguing in Publication Information Available

Library of Congress Cataloging-in-Publication Data

Putney, Martha S., 1916–
    When the nation was in need ; Blacks in the Women's Army Corps during World War II / by Martha S. Putney
        p.   cm.
    Includes bibliographical references and index.
    ISBN 0-8108-4017-0
    ISBN: 978-0-8108-4017-1

  1.   World War, 1939–1945—Participation, Afro-American.
  2.   United States. Army. Women's Army Corps—History.
  3.   World War, 1939–1945—Regimental Histories—United States. 4. United States. Army—Afro-American troops—History—20th century. I. Title.

Cloth edition copyright © 1992 by Martha S. Putney
D810-N4P88   1992
940.54'03—dc20
                            92-24084

DEDICATED TO

All the Black Women Who Served

in the Corps During World War II

and the

Memory of My Parents

CONTENTS

PREFACE

Women have rendered service with and given combat support to the United States Army since the birth of the nation. Some of them were "camp followers" and others cared for the sick and wounded, performing an assortment of tasks. Most of them remain anonymous. During the Civil War, Harriet Tubman (along with some other black women) served as a volunteer nurse at some army camps. Tubman also was a scout and a spy for the Union Army throughout the period of the Civil War. Dorothea Dix was the superintendent of women's nurses for the Union Army; she headed one of the first organized groups of women that assisted the nation's sick and wounded servicemen. Clara Barton was in charge of the Sanitary Commission which, like its successor, the Red Cross, rendered relief to the wounded and needy soldiers. But neither Tubman, nor other black females who labored at army camps, nor the women nurses under Dorothea Dix, nor the female Sanitary Commission workers, nor those who served before them were "in the army." Nor were they on the army payroll.

It was not until 1901 when the Army Nurse Corps was created by an act of Congress that the army officially opened its rolls to women—non-black women only. It took a widespread influenza epidemic during the closing years of World War I before the army was willing to accept black women into its volunteer nurses' corps; in December 1918, eighteen black women were permitted to join the nurses' corps. During World War I hundreds of women served with the army at home and with the American Expeditionary Force in France in such jobs as telephone operators, clerical workers, typists, stenographers, dietitians, and in quartermaster supply without the benefit of regular civil service status or of military status. They were not "in the army" either.

Moreover, none of the War Department's pre-World War II plans contemplated an organized, disciplined force of women. The military's view was that women did not belong in the army. It was not until war broke out in Europe in September 1939 that serious planning for a women's corps began. The Battle of Britain and the courageous role played by the British women's corps in the defense of that country won additional support in the U.S. military and in Congress for a women's corps. It was only after the attack on Pearl Harbor in December 1941 that the military brass and a majority in Congress were moved to support an organized, disciplined women's corps. And, then, only as an auxiliary to the army. Full military status for women did not come until September 1943, when the corps became an integral part of the Army of the United States.

Although Congress had rejected pleas by black organizations and leaders for the inclusion of a nondiscrimination clause in the legislation authorizing the auxiliary, Congress had a pledge from the War Department that blacks would be permitted to join the volunteer organization. Some 6,500 black women, including some 146 commissioned officers, served in the corps during World War II. But there were never more than 3,920 black enlisted women and 121 officers in the corps at any one time. They were assigned to duty stations at the training centers, in recruiting districts, on army posts, on army air force bases, at army hospitals, and overseas at a central postal battalion. This book is the story of those black women who volunteered and served in a sexually and racially segregated army during a period of global warfare.

The records at the National Archives and the Bethune Archives, the papers of the National Association for the Advancement of Colored People, fact sheets and reports at the Center of Military History in Washington, D.C., data prepared by the Women's Army Corps School at Fort McClellan, Alabama, and contemporary newspaper accounts were the main sources of information for this book. Interviews, statements, personal files, and letters of some of the women who served in the corps provided much additional information.

The writer wishes to thank those ex-service women who

made available their personal papers and related their military experiences, which shed light on some events and stories on which other sources were silent. The author is especially indebted to Dovey Johnson Roundtree, Ethel Heywood Smith, and Blanche L. Scott—three pioneers in the corps—and Eunice M. Wright, who joined the corps after World War II, for supplying valuable information. Many of the pictures contained herein came from the albums of Blanche L. Scott and Ethel Heywood Smith or from the files at the National Archives. Others were collected over the years by the author.

Martha S. Putney
Washington, D.C.

1. BLACKS AT WOMEN'S ARMY CORPS TRAINING CENTERS

The legislation creating the Women's Army Auxiliary Corps (WAAC), the organization's name from its inception until its incorporation into the Army of the United States on September 1, 1943, was introduced in Congress by Representative Edith Nourse Rogers of Massachusetts. Congress had approved the bill on May 14, 1942, and President Roosevelt signed it into law the same day. Oveta Culp Hobby of Houston, Texas, was sworn in as director of the organization on the same day the bill became law. She and army personnel began immediately at breakneck speed to get the corps operational. The urgency was no doubt related to the fortunes of the allied forces on the battlefields, which were none too bright at that time. In less than three months, on July 20, 1942, the first women to enter the WAAC arrived at Fort Des Moines (Iowa), the location of the First WAAC Training Center, to begin training as officers.[1]

The army had opened its doors to women other than nurses. It was energetically recruiting them for its auxiliary service; it was promising them equal pay with its men for comparable grades and ranks; and it was offering to involve them in every aspect of the military except the bearing of arms. It had also announced that its policy of racial segregation would be extended to its women's auxiliary.[2]

Forty blacks were among the 440 women who began training in July 1942. The number forty was no accident. The War Department, in seeking the legislation, had promised Congress that it would enroll blacks up to 10.6 percent of the WAAC's strength, a percentage roughly equivalent to the proportion of blacks in the total population. The quota apparently was designed to ensure that blacks did not exceed

1

that number. Even in the men's army at the onset of World War II, the Selective Service had sent directives to some of its offices in the field not to recruit blacks.[3] No other ethnic group in the United States, a nation of ethnics, was subjected to a publicly announced quota for the army.

Even with the quota, the army had a hard time assembling the forty qualified black females for the charter group of WAACs. Army personnel made last-minute "hurried trips to Negro Colleges to attempt to recruit" some of the forty. These last-minute efforts apparently were made to ward off embarrassment from black leaders and organizations and some non-black agencies who had warned the army that not many qualified blacks were likely to volunteer for a segregated corps.[4]

The army evidently felt that it had taken care of this problem when it brought in Mary McLeod Bethune, founding president of Bethune-Cookman College and president of the National Council of Negro Women, as an unofficial advisor to help recruit and select the forty black women. The War Department had rejected a recommendation that Bethune, who was a friend of the then first lady, Eleanor Roosevelt, be commissioned by direct appointment as an assistant director of the WAAC. Her age (sixty-seven) was given as the reason for rejection. Her age likewise disqualified her from enrolling in the corps—the age requirement being from twenty to fifty.[5]

Why These Forty Blacks Joined the WAAC

In their formal applications, the forty successful applicants, all handpicked and approved by Bethune, gave a variety of reasons for joining. Among these reasons was one common theme: in their own words the women stated that they could not stand aside while their brothers, husbands, boyfriends, male relatives, and other Americans were fighting or when the nation needed help. This was the official rationale which they gave.[6]

Behind these written statements, almost certainly, must have been the exhortation of Bethune in her call for "One

Black WAAC." She knew that if one black joined, others would follow. She was aware that women throughout the world at war were in the struggle for freedom and that black American females should not sit this one out. She was aware that the official war propaganda implicitly and explicitly posited a change. The nation had proclaimed itself the "arsenal of democracy." Its foes were fascism, totalitarianism, Aryan supremacy, and the "Yellow Peril." She worked hard to convince black women that they had to "reach out to share in the struggle." Bethune saw in the WAAC an opportunity for black females not only to help the nation in its hour of need but also to share in the fruits of victory. She stressed the benefits of being in the service. She spoke in terms of democracy, equality, improved race relations, women's rights, and employment opportunities. Her hope was for a United States with equal justice and equal opportunity for all of its citizens.[7]

In the United States of the early 1940s, racism—legal and de facto—was a way of life. It was only after years of protests and the threat of a march on Washington by A. Philip Randolph, president of the Brotherhood of Sleeping Car Porters and Maids, that a reluctant Franklin Roosevelt in June 1941 signed an executive order establishing the Fair Employment Practice Committee. Despite the executive order and the committee, fairness in employment did not exist in governmental and nongovernmental workplaces.[8]

In the federal bureaucracy (except for a handful of show-pieces, scattered here and there in the various agencies, who owed their highfalutin titles and powerless positions to politics), blacks were relegated to the jobs of laborers, janitors, chairwomen, messengers, chauffeurs, low-level clerks, and, belatedly, elevator operators. One wag stated that there were more blacks with law degrees in the post office in Washington, working as mail handlers, truck drivers, and letter carriers, than there were practicing black lawyers in the whole of the United States. In the nonpublic workplaces, especially in the defense industries, the anti-black policy also existed; blacks were permitted to take jobs that non-blacks did not want. At the same time, large numbers of women had left their traditional place in the home and entered the workforce, in the defense plants, factories, mills, offices, and on the assembly lines, as the men went off to war.

In matters related to the military, the section of the Selective Service and Training Act of 1940 that prohibited discrimination in the selection and training of men was ignored. The civilian bureaucrats in charge of the Selective Service boards and their military advisors decided whom they would accept and by implication how these men would be used in the military. Some boards selected only non-black men. Colonel Benjamin C. Davis, Sr., then the highest-ranking black in the army, who had been passed over on the promotion list (the military's way of forcing an individual into retirement), obtained his one star (brigadier general rank) because of black protest and the need to keep blacks in the fold of the Democratic party for the 1940 election. For generally the same reasons, a black was added as an assistant to the selective service director and another as an assistant to the secretary of war.[9]

These last two actions were merely smoke screens; neither the man in the office of the director of selective service nor the assistant in the office of the secretary of war had any substantive authority or power. Despite Pearl Harbor and the herculean effort required to gain the initiative on the war fronts in the Pacific, Europe, and North Africa, the War Department proclaimed again and again that the army was not going to be "a social laboratory."[10]

The army, thus, had declared publicly its adherence to the policy of segregation, and it did not take long for those forty blacks in the first Officer Candidate School (OCS) class to learn that the army meant what it said. On the very first day, one of the male officers who met the 440 women greeted them by yelling: "Negroes on one side! White girls on the other!" One of the commissioned officers who was standing nearby reportedly remarked that he had had no dealings with educated blacks, that he had only known "razor-cutting Negroes," and that he supposed that they were all the same. Later, in a class lecture, one of the army instructors was quoted as using the term "razor-cutting Negroes" again.[11]

Other blacks who subsequently arrived at Fort Des Moines as enlisted women for basic training likewise felt the sting of segregation. As they alighted one-by-one in front of post headquarters from army trucks bringing them from the depot in the city of Des Moines, the officer of the day checked off their names and directed them to line up at one location; the whites who arrived with them were directed to another location. This was the point, at the entrance to Fort Des Moines in front of post headquarters while still in civilian clothes, at which segregation for blacks began in the WAAC. The Chinese-Americans, Native Americans, Puerto Ricans, Filipino-Americans, and all other ethnic Americans were lumped together in integrated units. Blacks were set apart. The only exception to this arrangement was one Puerto Rican unit which, according to the official historian, existed not because of ethnic origin but because of the language barrier. However, some Afro-Puerto Ricans presented the authorities at Fort Des Moines with a dilemma. The authorities wanted to place them with the blacks. These Afro-Puerto Ricans did not want to be with the blacks; they insisted on being in units with the other Puerto Ricans and that is where they were placed.[12] These Puerto Ricans may have been in the same unit that the official historian stated existed only because of a language barrier.

The Training Centers and Their Programs

In addition to Fort Des Moines, the corps subsequently opened centers at Daytona Beach (Florida), Fort Oglethorpe (Georgia), Fort Devens (Massachusetts), and a fifth one with its headquarters and one section in Ruston (Louisiana) and a section each at Camp Polk (Louisiana) and Monticello (Arkansas). Some of these centers maintained programs other than basic training. Fort Des Moines, for example, had an officer candidate school, an intermediate officer school, an opportunity school, and a special training unit. Fort Des Moines also had an administration school, cooks and bakers school, and a motor transport school, which were located off-post in the city of Des Moines. Fort Oglethorpe began an officer candidate school in July 1943, and before it was closed down in July 1945 had an intermediate officer school and a program for training medical, surgical, and dental technicians and medical clerks. More women took their training at Fort Des Moines than at any other center. Some 56,000 went through Fort Des Moines, while Fort Oglethorpe had about 53,000. The Daytona Beach center serviced about 28,000; Fort Devens, 5,000; and the center headquartered at Ruston, 1,300.[13]

It appears that the army and the corps had decided early to avoid as much as possible the training of blacks at the three centers located in the Southern states. This inference is drawn from the rationale the corps used to support the decision to close down the training programs at Fort Oglethorpe rather than at Fort Des Moines (to be discussed later in this chapter), the statement of the director of the corps in February 1943 that one black group was to stay as a training center complement at Fort Des Moines and one at Fort Devens, and the circumstance that few, if any, blacks were sent to Daytona Beach or any of the locations of the fifth center for training. Probably the only blacks who were trained at Fort Oglethorpe were those specifically recruited in late 1944 and early 1945 for assignment in army general hospitals and some of the black officers who were commissioned between September 18, 1943, and February 17, 1945. The training operations at Fort Devens were terminated in August 1943 after only six months and the personnel (including 21 officers and 589 enlisted women) were transferred to Fort Des Moines.[14] Hence, it would seem that a majority of the blacks received their training at the center at Fort Des Moines.

Blacks were enrolled in every program at the training centers. All of them took the basic training course or a modified version of it; fewer of them were enrolled in the other programs. All of the women, both black and non-black, in a specific program had virtually the same course of study. From time to time, however, the length of the program varied either to meet the needs of the service or to improve the quality of the training. For example, a four-week basic training course was first extended to six weeks and later to eight weeks. An initial officer candidate school program of six weeks was extended to eight weeks, reduced to six weeks, and finally extended to twelve weeks. During most of the

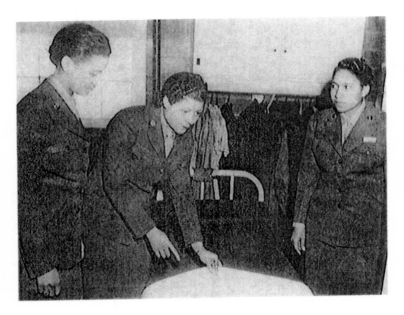

Top: Recruits boarding army truck en route to basic training center. *Bottom:* Instructing trainees on how to make a bed, army style.

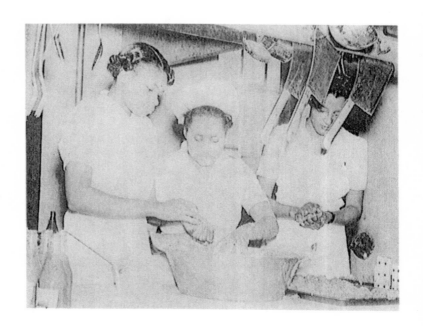

Top: Food preparation at the cooks and bakers school. *Bottom:* Basic training completed; WACs on their way to field assignments.

period, the Army Service Forces was in charge of the direction and coordination of the programs. The medical recruits—those destined for assignments at army general hospitals—were under the direct supervision of the medical department and took an abbreviated basic training course followed by a six-week medical course. They were taught by doctors, nurses, and enlisted medical technicians. As early as June 1944, a black Women's Army Corps Physical Therapy Medical Technician School was established at the station hospital at Fort Huachuca (Arizona), which was similar to a segment of the program at the Medical Department Enlisted Technician School at Wakeman General Hospital at Camp Atterbury (Indiana).[15]

An Opportunity School was opened at Fort Des Moines in August 1943 for those women who had completed basic training but who had no usable military skills and who because of "lack of ability and/or aptitude" did not qualify for specialist training. The director of the corps received periodic reports on the status of the students in Opportunity School and those in the Special Training Unit which was begun at Fort Des Moines in April 1944 and was designed to provide pre-basic training primarily in academic areas for those who scored low on the Army General Classification Test (AGCT).[16]

The enrollment in Opportunity School and the Special Training Unit at times exceeded 100, but there were usually more students in the latter program. After a period of training, many in the Opportunity School were transferred to field assignments and occasionally to Cooks and Bakers School. For example, the report of July 1, 1944, showed that 19 non-black and 10 black women were sent to field assignments and 1 non-black was sent to Cooks and Bakers School. Two weeks later, 5 blacks and 16 non-blacks were transferred to the field. During the course of its operation, the Special Training Unit enrolled 426 enlisted women, including 83 blacks. Of these, 345 (including 66 blacks) were transferred to the regular basic training program. And 17 blacks and 64 non-blacks in the program were discharged from the service.[17]

A singular feature about Opportunity School and the

Special Training Unit was that blacks and non-blacks were at times mixed together in the same company. At least one black commissioned officer was assigned as executive officer (the second in command) of a company in Opportunity School. A Special Training Unit had a black commissioned officer as its plans and training officer, and a black non-commissioned officer as one of its platoon sergeants. This latter unit was composed of four or five blacks, a few Hispanics, and the rest were mainstream non-black ethnics. When these two units were activated, integration of the swimming pool automatically followed since time slots for use of the pool were assigned by unit designation. Shortly thereafter, the whole system of segregated swimming broke down.[18] The picture on page 11 shows a mixed Special Training Unit company participating in a ceremonial parade at Fort Des Moines in May 1945. The picture was taken by the post photographer. If released to the press, it would have given an incorrect impression. Opportunity School and the Special Training Unit were atypical in their ethnic composition, probably the only two of their kind in the WAC or even in the entire army at that time.

Earlier at Fort Des Moines, when the staging area (the place where enlisted women were quartered to await assignment or further training) had become crowded, an attempt to mix black and non-black women in the same barracks created a problem. Some non-blacks refused to sleep under the same roof as blacks and walked out. At that time, the total number of people at Fort Des Moines was almost 9,000, while the capacity at the post was 6,050. Some non-blacks at the Administration School at the Chamberlain Hotel in the city of Des Moines grumbled about having to live in the same building and being assigned to the same kitchen police (KP) shift as blacks. Reports of these grumblings reached some members of Congress, the War Department, the press, the post commander, and some of the officers and enlisted personnel on the post. Under the rallying call of "forced mixing," an effort was made to resist any breach in the wall of segregation. Stories in the press, especially the Southern press, decried the "forcing" of these "fine and virtuous white ladies" to eat, do KP, and live with blacks. The few blacks at

A racially mixed Special Training Unit in a ceremonial parade at Fort Des Moines, May 1945. (Photo by post photographer)

the Administration School (who were there to learn how the army did its paperwork) were lodged on a separate floor, apart from the others.[19] Apparently, the sleeping arrangement was not changed at the Chamberlain Hotel.

Earlier, in the latter part of 1942, some black basic trainees at Fort Des Moines had initiated a movement to desegregate the mess hall. The inspiration for their action probably stemmed from the circumstance that on Saturdays and Sundays they proceeded to the mess hall on their own and felt that they should not voluntarily segregate themselves. Obviously, their action did not sit well with some non-blacks or with the acting post commandant. About the same time, one or two "liberal" non-blacks began to drop into the black service club and to partake of refreshments with the blacks.

Immediately, post headquarters had notices placed on bulletin boards ordering an end to the mingling of the races in the mess hall and the service club. However, a number of events occurred which precluded any effective implementation of the post commander's orders. First, a staff officer from the War Department importuned the acting commandant to remove the signs from the bulletin boards and suggested that "Desegregation Days" in the mess hall might serve to improve race relations. OCS was desegregated in November 1942, and the blacks at the school were alphabetically scattered among their classmates at seats in the mess hall. And the acting commandant, who was reportedly ailing, was removed from his post at Fort Des Moines.[20] What started out as "putting one over on whitey" on Saturdays and Sundays became the practice at Fort Des Moines on these days of the week. And non-blacks who had a mind to do so could break bread with blacks at the black service club.

With few exceptions at Fort Des Moines and with no exceptions at Fort Devens, black officers were assigned as company cadre regardless of their talents, skills, abilities, or previous experience. One of the exceptions at Fort Des Moines was Mary L. Lewis, a former home economics teacher and a member of the first OCS class. Lewis finished the army's mess officers school and was assigned to the mess hall. Her duties were to plan menus and to write up instructions for mess management. However, Lewis did not last long on this job and, for a while at least, found herself as a commander of a staging area company to which she was apparently ill suited. Another exception was the officers assigned to the black service club. Charity E. Adams, who had been a public school teacher in Columbia, South Carolina, prior to entering the service with the first OCS class, was a company commander during most of her time at Fort Des Moines. When she was promoted to the rank of major in September 1943, she became the highest-ranking black WAC at Fort Des Moines and the second-highest-ranking black officer in the corps. Adams described herself as a company commander, a staff training officer, and a station control officer at Fort Des Moines. A newspaper report at the time of her promotion to major referred to her as a supervisor of plans and training at headquarters at Fort Des Moines.[21]

As company cadre of black troops at the training centers, the black officers' job was not only to see their troops through basic training but also to enhance their self-esteem, self-worth, and pride. The sentiment common among the black cadre was that the latter was just as important (if not more so) than the former because of society's perception of them as inferior. Vera G. Campbell, a member of the first OCS class and a company commander at Fort Des Moines, was by training and practice a successful podiatrist in New York City, and she felt that the army would have had an urgent need for individuals with her skills. In joining the corps, she looked forward to practicing her specialty in the service. Campbell's challenge to her troops, and the challenge of others who found themselves in a similar situation, was to do the best that they could in whatever job the army assigned them.[22]

Speaking of her assignment in the WAC and that of other black officers at the training center, Campbell said that they did not need to exhort, cajole, or intimidate the troops to get them to understand how by doing well they could help themselves as individuals and blacks as a race and at the same time help the nation win the war. She added that the fact that the women (almost without exception) entered the service looking for something better or wanting to do well was a big plus. Campbell said that the company officers she knew were a dedicated group of women and their troops at the end of the training period were disciplined, poised, physically fit, self-confident, and knowledgeable in basic military lore, rules, and regulations.[23]

Ina McRae, a platoon sergeant regarded by some as one of the premier drill sergeants at Fort Des Moines, talked of the dedication of the black cadre and its determined effort to bring out the best in the women. She also spoke of the willingness and eagerness of the women to learn. She said that it was a pleasure to have worked with them.[24]

The black officers at Fort Des Moines did not always agree on issues affecting the race. Disagreement was publicly displayed in a meeting concerning a reorganization plan. On August 23, 1943, headquarters at Fort Des Moines circulated a memorandum on the formation of an all-black regiment. According to the plan, all of the blacks on the post were to have been placed under the command of the regiment, a sort of South African-style black "homeland." The memorandum directed the designated black regimental officers to "report to and understudy white officers now performing [those] duties." The designated black regimental commander was instructed to "work with the TC [Training Center] Classification Officer" in the selection of "suitably trained colored cadre . . . in sufficient time before the transformation to insure that companies taken over from white officers are properly administered." The reorganization was to have become operational on September 1, 1943, a date which coincided with the conversion of the Women's Army Auxiliary Corps to the Women's Army Corps.[25] (See Appendix 7.)

A month of rumors and off-the-record talks had preceded the memorandum. During this period, some of the black officers and enlisted women had problems with the plan. They held that the barriers separating the races on the post were already too visible, that the plan was a step toward more isolation, and that the further isolation would heighten the misperception of black inferiority. They argued that the plan ran counter to the very things the United States was fighting the war for. They took issue with those among them who felt that the plan would afford some with administrative and staff positions and hence promotions. They asserted that many company commanders were still first lieutenants when the rank of captain was authorized for that position; moreover, the critics declared that a few promotions were too high a price to pay for the damage that would have been done to racial aspirations. After the plan was officially announced, some officers and enlisted women publicly expressed their concerns about the reorganization, and were met with a statement that post headquarters had assurances that this was what the majority of the blacks wanted since it would provide them with assignments and experience in administrative and staff positions.[26]

At a meeting called to instruct the black officers on the proper procedures to be followed for the turning over and receiving of property, records, and funds for the units involved in the transfer, Captain Dovey M. Johnson rose to ask if questions were in order. Instead of a simple affirmative or negative reply, she got a gruff reception and was told, in effect, that this was a done deal. Whereupon, to the bewilderment of headquarters officials and amid mutterings from the assembled officers, three others immediately stood to be recognized. The first of the three wanted to know what her status would be if she did not participate in the scheduled mass swearing-in ceremony for the conversion of the WAAC to the WAC. The second objected to the plan "since people in some quarters are under the mistaken impression that this reorganization is desired by [the] majority of us." The third stated that she did not think that the plan met with the approval of most of the blacks.[27]

Noting that headquarters officers were somewhat taken aback by the remarks of the three officers, Captain Johnson rose to speak, taking off her insignia of rank to indicate her willingness to resign or accept discharge from the corps for what she was about to say. She spoke of the absence of racial incidents on the post and the progress that had been made in building interracial goodwill. She declared that the creation of the regiment would be a step backward and wondered aloud whether the benefit expected would outweigh the damage done to race relations. She stated that if the lessons taught to her and other WAACs by the training films *Four Freedoms* and *Why We Are Fighting* were to have any meaning, then the regiment should not exist. It was an emotional speech, and

Johnson practically preached to the group. When she finished, the meeting was summarily dismissed.[28]

Four days later, post headquarters circulated the statement shown on page 17.

The Detroit office of the National Association for the Advancement of Colored People reported that two captains and five first lieutenants had offered their resignations rather than accept the black unit. The National Council of Negro Women (of which Mary McLeod Bethune was a charter member) had opposed the reorganization plan and had made known its views to the office of the director of the corps, and this apparently aided in bringing about the plan's demise. In talking about the incident many years later, Johnson said that she was proud of whatever role she had played in the defeat of the implementation of the reorganization.[29]

That both the announcement of the creation of the all-black regiment and the cancellation of the project were circulated in the form of unnumbered memorandums seems to indicate that the scheme was of local origin. It may have been a sincere effort by the post commander, Colonel Frank U. McCoskrie, to provide blacks with administrative and staff job experience within the framework of a segregated corps and in keeping with War Department guidelines to confine blacks to company work. The willingness of Colonel McCoskrie to abandon the project when he became aware of its unpopularity among some officers seems to indicate his desire not to impair the morale of blacks, also evident in the position he took on the black band, an issue that will be discussed in Chapter 3.

Off-Duty Activities

The main center for off-duty activities for enlisted women at Fort Des Moines was the segregated service club where there were games, music, a reading room, a refreshments bar, and space for dancing. A good bit of the dancing, however, was sole or exhibition since there were no black men assigned to the post. The several units of men stationed there—the military police, the instructional staff, the medical corpsmen and doctors, the quartermaster personnel, the motor pool

HEADQUARTERS[30]
FIRST WOMEN'S ARMY CORPS TRAINING CENTER
FORT DES MOINES, IOWA

CJC:rh
4 September, 1943

MEMORANDUM:

TO   :   All concerned.

Unnumbered memorandum this headquarters, 23 August, 1943 pertaining to conversion of 3rd Regiment from mixed white and colored to a colored Regiment, is revoked.

By order of Colonel McCOSKRIE:

C. J. Crumm
Capt., AGD,
Adjutant

DISTRIBUTION
   1 Each 1st and 3rd Regts.
   1 Each 4th Bn 3rd Regt.
   1 Each Officer Named in Par 5.
   1 Each Personnel
   1 Each Classification
   1 Director of Training
   1 School Mess Officer
   1 Billeting Officer
   1 Post Engineer
   1 Post Quartermaster
   1 WAAC Supply
   1 Surgeon

specialists, headquarters staff, and chaplains and their assistants—were all non-black. The forty or so black soldiers who had been stationed at Fort Des Moines prior to the coming of the first OCS class in July 1942 were transferred to Fort Dodge (Iowa) within a day or so after the women arrived. On some weekends, though, a few enlisted men (mainly from Fort Dodge and the Naval Air Station at Ottumwa, Iowa) and some male civilians (mainly from the local Des Moines area) made their way to the black service club on the post. But there were never enough dancing partners for the women who crowded into the club.[31]

The black women at Fort Devens not only had their own social and recreational area but also—individually and collectively at the invitations of the members of the all-black 372nd Infantry Regiment, which was stationed at Fort Devens— shared in the social and recreational activities of the regiment. On at least one occasion, reportedly, the regiment's black commanding officer, Colonel Queen, went to the WAC office to solicit the attendance of particular enlisted women at a dance when there was some reluctance on the part of the WAC's company commander to permit the women to attend. Colonel Queen and his staff had earlier issued a standing invitation to the women to attend regimental social functions.[32]

The non-segregated theater at Fort Des Moines, the tennis courts in season, use of the swimming pool by schedule, and a bicycle rental stand just outside the post provided various forms of entertainment and recreation for the women. Both at Fort Des Moines and at Fort Devens, the black WACs enjoyed the amenities of the local communities, especially the black communities. They attended the black churches. Some had dinners in the homes of the local residents.[33]

The black officers at Fort Des Moines—usually there were more there than anywhere else—had little or no social life. Although they lived among the post's aristocracy on officers' row in Cape Cod-style homes around the spacious parade grounds, they were socially apart from the rest of the residents of that bedroom community; they formed black enclaves which were geographically a part of the group yet socially isolated from it. The social isolation was total except for one or two who played cards at the nurses' quarters, an occasional greeting in passing or brief conversations in the post exchange or theater. Some few, however, met friends in the city of Des Moines or in Chicago on weekend or longer leaves. On the other hand, although housed in the company area with enlisted women in a less than homelike setting, black officers at Fort Devens did have other black officers on the post. Hence they did not experience the sense of isolation, of being cut off from social contact, that those at Fort Des Moines felt.[34]

Placing the officers club off-limits to black officers at Fort Des Moines yet permitting prisoners of war access to the club was a source of irritation to most blacks. This irritation changed to bewilderment when Bethune made an inspection tour. Curiously, the commandant arranged a dinner for her at the officers club. According to the papers in the Bethune Archives, Bethune was concerned about reports of discriminatory treatment of blacks, and she wanted to visit some army posts to assess the situation. The War Department staff in Washington had advised the commandant at Fort Des Moines to accommodate her and to dispel her concerns. During her visit, Bethune, at times escorted by black officers and at other times escorted by members of the post headquarters staff, went everywhere on the post—everywhere except the officers club. The black officers had told her that they were barred from the club, and Bethune probably mentioned this to the commandant. The commandant may also have suspected that Bethune was aware of the army regulation that clubs located on federal property were to be open to all officers assigned to that facility.[35]

Then, to just about everyone's surprise, the invitation came. Dressed in army "pinks" (then the ceremonial garb for officers), Captain Dovey Johnson took Bethune to the door of the club and stood at attention saluting other officers when Bethune hesitated, expecting Johnson to accompany her inside. Bethune had to be reminded that black officers had orders not to enter the club. Reportedly, Bethune (with the commandant seated next to her at the table) talked the whole time about "her" black WACs. The commandant was said to have been so taken aback by the substance of her remarks that

Mail call—one of the best calls in the WAC.

he did not eat his meal. Bethune broke the color bar at the officers club at Fort Des Moines, but the club remained off-limits to black officers.[36]

Without an official place on the post to entertain their male guests, some officers (with the tacit consent of, others with the informal approval of, and still others with the knowledge of all or most of their housemates) invited their male guests to their quarters.[37] Since the army had a long-standing policy of non-fraternization between officers and enlisted personnel, officers who entertained enlisted men, especially in quarters on army posts, placed themselves in a potentially precarious position. The non-fraternization policy was premised on the concept that familiarity breeds contempt. Three officers suffered the consequences of this policy.

Officials at post headquarters and non-black officers in nearby houses had observed enlisted men entering and leaving at least one residence. They were, apparently, reluctant to initiate the charges, but one accuser did bring formal charges against three of her black housemates after she had been reprimanded by the senior officer in charge of her quarters for urinating on the floor while she was inebriated and then refusing to clean up the mess when she became sober. According to the court record, the accuser cussed out the senior officer and named people at post headquarters who had wanted her to sign formal charges. Once she signed the charges, the authorities at post headquarters prepared to convene a general court-martial.[38]

The three officers—Captain Frances A. Futrell, Second Lieutenant Margaret A. Curtis, and Second Lieutenant Gladys E. Pace—were charged with several specifications of associating with enlisted men in the quarters under the provisions of the Ninety-sixth Article of War, a section of the document that is tantamount to a constitution for the military. The Ninety-sixth Article, a general, catchall clause, reads:

Mary McLeod Bethune visiting a WAC unit.

Though not mentioned in these articles, all disorders and neglects to the prejudice of good order and military discipline, all conduct of a nature to bring discredit upon the military service, and all crimes or offenses not capital, of which persons subject to military law may be guilty, shall be taken cognizance of by a general or special or summary court-martial according to the nature and degree of the offense, and punished at the discretion of such court.[39]

The record of the trial clearly shows that the accuser, Second Lieutenant Aubrey A. Stokes, had approved of entertaining the enlisted men in the quarters and had participated in the entertainment. The enlisted men, who were sailors stationed at the Naval Air Station in Ottumwa, Iowa, and others at the trial attested to this.[40]

Before the trial began, each of the accused officers was given the option of resigning from the WAC for the good of the service. They and their defense team decided to proceed with the trial. Their decision was apparently based on a number of factors. First, the accuser was herself a participant in the activities on which the charges were based. Second, their quarters were the only place on the post where black officers could entertain guests; they were barred from the officers club, and the service club was for enlisted personnel. Third, other officers on the post had entertained enlisted men in their quarters. And fourth, a friend of the accused who was to be a witness for the prosecution allegedly had a "bad reputation."[41]

The court consisted of ten officers; none was below the rank of captain and one was a WAC. The trial lasted three days, from January 8 to January 10, 1945. By a two-thirds secret written ballot, Captain Futrell was found guilty of eight of the nine specifications and the charge of violating the Ninety-sixth Article of War, and was sentenced to dismissal from the service. By the same vote, Lieutenant Curtis was found guilty of all six specifications and the charge of violating the Ninety-sixth Article of War. By a similar vote, Lieutenant Pace was found guilty of four of the six specifications and the charge of violating the Ninety-sixth Article of War. Lieutenants Curtis and Pace were each sentenced to forfeit fifty dollars a month for twelve months. The case was sent through channels for review, and the sentences were approved. Subsequently, Lieutenant Pace requested and received permission to resign "without specification as to the character thereof which implies neither an honorable nor dishonorable separation."[42] It is not known whether Lieutenant Curtis requested or received the same permission.

It seems that authorities pursued the case in order to put an end to the socializing between black officers and black enlisted men on the post. Captain Futrell stated when interrogated at the trial that the problem never came up at Fort Huachuca (Arizona), where she had been stationed previously, and where there were 15,000 black enlisted men and 600 black male officers. At Fort Des Moines and its surrounding area black male officers were practically nonexistent. Post authorities could have achieved the same goal if anywhere along the line they had told just one black officer to stop socializing with enlisted men. She would have broadcast the order, and an order in the military is a command.

The larger question which a number of WACs, both black and non-black, confronted before and after this case was how valid was the military's insistence on social distance between commissioned officers and enlisted personnel now that a substantial number of women were in the service. The director of the corps had been aware of the larger question and had had it under study at least as early as June 1943.[43] She did not consider, however, that it was desirable "to lay down a categorical policy or rule," believing that the social distance between enlisted personnel and officers should follow the norm that prevailed in civilian life between employer and employee, and should show good judgment and common sense. She did not push for a definitive modification of the policy.[44]

Problems were cropping up in the field, and the people at headquarters in Washington became more concerned with the matter. Several statements were drafted but none was issued although it was admitted that existing "conditions [of women in the army] might dictate some departure from the normal customs." But the policymakers did not believe "a complete relaxation" was "either indicated or desirable."

Above: Some of the first groups of blacks to arrive at Fort Des Moines for basic training in 1942.

Opposite: One of the last black basic training units at Fort Des Moines.

Company 5, 3rd Reg., First WAC Training Center, Fort Des Moines, Iowa, 20 January, 1945
1st Lt. Tretha B. Brown, Commanding Officer — 2nd Lt. Julia H. Williams, Second in Command
2nd Lt. Idalina M. Moore, Supply and Recreational Officer

Hence, local commands were told that the "literal observance of the custom was impractical . . . in non-official or private activities."[45]

Nothing in the record of the case of the three black officers shows that either the defense team or members of the court were aware of the discretion given to local commanders on the matter of fraternization. The prosecution, of course, did not bring up the matter. Local commanders were aware of it as early as January 1944, and this case was not tried until a year later. Would the knowledge by at least the defense team that the "literal observance of the custom was impractical" have made a difference in the outcome of the case?

As a result of entrusting to local commanders the determination of what was permissible "in non-official or private social activities," some enlisted women were court-martialed for fraternizing with officers. The director was made aware of some instances in April 1944, and apparently could do nothing to change the situation. She also approved of the sentence given to Captain Futrell.[46]

Colonel Westray B. Boyce, who succeeded Hobby as director, thought that the absence of an announced War Department policy on fraternization "led to inevitable and unfortunate inequality in handling the problem," which Boyce regarded as "probably the second strongest adverse factor in WAC morale." The policy, she declared, should have been made and announced at the War Department level to prevent "inequality among commands." Boyce noted that Hobby had recommended that the army consider a modification of its accepted policy "in the case of men and women when not on Army posts." Boyce's pronouncement was in the form of a memorandum entitled "For Anyone Writing History."[47] It seems, then, that the military bureaucracy resisted the change, and that the army was rooted in its customs and traditions.

In late 1944, the War Department contemplated consolidating the WAC basic training program in one location. Fort Devens had been closed in August 1943. The center with its headquarters at Ruston, Louisiana, had been closed in June 1943, and the Daytona Beach center was deactivated a year later. In deciding whether to retain Fort Oglethorpe or Fort

Des Moines, it was judged that the former had the advantage of size, climate, and better transportation facilities to off-post activities for the women. On the other hand, Fort Des Moines was regarded as more centrally located and hence more accessible from all sections of the country. Moreover, Fort Des Moines was considered a better location for the training of blacks since Chattanooga, Tennessee—the urban area close to Fort Oglethorpe—offered little for blacks during their off-duty hours. The civilian advisory committee, which had been appointed by the War Department, had warned that "negro women in uniform are not as well received as men in the South." So Fort Des Moines remained a training center until all training activities ended on December 15, 1945.[48]

The overwhelming majority of black WACs who served during World War II were stationed at Fort Des Moines at one time or another. Large numbers took their basic training there; some went to administration school or cooks and bakers school or motor transport school there. All but a few of the black officers went to OCS there. Other blacks began their military service at Fort Devens, where black officers served exclusively as company cadre. Those assigned to Fort Des Moines were for the most part company officers, and with a few exceptions they worked with black troops. Some few were in special service and recreational work, one was briefly a mess officer, and one was a staff training officer. Fort Des Moines was the home base for officers in an attached unassigned status who were between duty assignments or were awaiting assignments. Neither at Fort Des Moines nor at Fort Devens nor at Fort Oglethorpe did they find life uneventful. More than a few who were at Fort Des Moines would probably agree with a black enlisted woman who said that she found conditions there "pretty fair" when compared with other camps at which she subsequently was stationed.[49]

2. RECRUITMENT

After what appeared to have been a herculean effort to enroll blacks who met its standards, the WAAC/WAC put black recruitment on a back burner. Knowledgeable organizations and black leaders had warned the army and the WAAC that their segregation policy would have a negative effect on their efforts to enroll the better-qualified blacks for a volunteer corps. A sustained effort in early 1943 to recruit a significant number of Japanese-Americans to serve as translators or at the Military Intelligence Language School fell far short of its goal, in large part probably because of the cultural orientation of the Japanese that women should not be in the military. The gigantic effort to recruit other ethnic Americans met with early success but then hit a number of snags including bad press and the failure of military men to accept in good faith a women's army. The corps spent a large amount of its energy and considerable funds to counter those negative influences.[1]

Requirements for enrollment in the corps were listed in brochures available at army recruiting offices and post offices, appeared in press notices and newspaper articles, and were read in radio broadcasts. To be eligible to join, a woman had to be a citizen of the United States, have two years of high school, be between twenty and forty-nine years old, have no dependents under age fourteen, and attain a satisfactory rating on a military aptitude test. The high school requirement was waived if the aptitude test score showed equivalent ability. The aptitude test most frequently given was the Army General Classification Test. Additionally, a successful applicant had to pass a physical examination and undergo an interview.[2]

Responding to questions by black leaders at her first press conference before the organization became operational, the director of the corps announced that two of the first eight companies of enlisted women to enter the WAAC would be black. At the same time, the director stated that the WAAC "will have the same liberal policy with respect to Negroes that exists in the Army." Those black leaders knew what the army's "liberal policy" was and they predicted then and there that the policy of segregation would discourage qualified blacks from joining.[3]

The Southern Negro Youth Congress, whose headquarters was in Birmingham, Alabama, sent a letter to Colonel Hobby on June 8, 1942, expressing the opposition of blacks to a segregated organization and urging a fully integrated corps and equality of treatment. The National Council of Negro Women declared in a report to the War Department that the best way to promote the recruitment of the better-qualified blacks was to make the "greatest use of [their] individual skills and abilities" and to have them "work within the framework of democracy."[4]

Several organizations, including the National Association for the Advancement of Colored People (NAACP), the National Urban League, the National Board of the Young Women's Christian Association, and the Rosenwald Fund sent committees or representatives to Fort Des Moines during the early life of the WAAC to make on-the-spot reports. All of them concluded that the corps would not attract the better-qualified blacks, and, they so advised the War Department.[5]

Colonel Hobby had joined the efforts of the army recruiters who went to black colleges searching for recruits for the first OCS class. On July 2, 1942, less than twenty days before the first OCS class arrived at Fort Des Moines to begin training, she spoke to a sorority at Howard University in Washington, D.C. Apparently, neither Director Hobby nor the army recruiters who "made hurried trips to Negro colleges" to enlist some members of the first OCS class knew that some recruiting stations were denying applications to some of the blacks who wanted to apply. A recruiter in Charlotte, North Carolina, refused to give an application to Dovey Johnson, and Bethune advised her to try to obtain one in Richmond, Virginia. The executive editor of the *Pittsburgh*

Courier advised the director's office that blacks could not obtain applications in Pittsburgh, Pennsylvania. It was also found that such other cities as Winston-Salem, Columbia, St. Paul, and Dallas had withheld applications from blacks.[6]

Later, in the latter part of 1942, acknowledging only that segregation may have been a cause for the failure of more qualified blacks to enroll, the corps, through the army, proceeded to obfuscate the issue. It claimed that a War Department policy statement on the matter would remove segregation as a deterrent to black enlistment. The policy statement, issued in late 1942, read as follows:

> There is a definite reluctance on the part of the best qualified colored women to volunteer in the WAAC. This is brought about by an impression on their part that they will not be well received or treated on posts where they may be stationed. This could be overcome by an intensive recruiting campaign with the idea in view of interesting the desired class of colored women in the project and arriving at a thorough understanding of their rights and privileges while in the service. . . . An eminently qualified person, preferably a Negro recruiter, will be sent out to colored colleges in order to secure the proper class of applicants.[7]

Nothing in this statement explicitly mentioned the segregation policy. Since there was some reluctance on the part of non-blacks to enroll for other reasons (such as the persistent rumors of their becoming social companions for the servicemen), this statement, with the deletion of the words "colored" and "Negro," could very well have applied to anyone.

More to the point, in the view of many blacks, no amount of persuasion by recruiters could induce a representative number of the better-qualified blacks to join. Too many of them had experienced firsthand or knew someone who had experienced the dehumanizing effects of segregation, had read in the press or heard firsthand accounts of the mistreatment of blacks, and the horror tales emanating from the South. They also had heard or read of black servicemen in uniform being set upon, beaten, and maimed by local police, or mobs, or both. Many Northern blacks in particular, although they had experienced some forms of de facto segregation, were completely turned off by the Southern style of race relations.

Curiously, both in regard to obtaining applicants to round out the first forty to enter OCS and subsequently to bringing in "the proper class of applicants," recruiters were directed to the "colored colleges." Most of these colleges were in the South, and almost all of their students were preparing for careers as nurses, teachers, school administrators, social workers, doctors, lawyers, and agricultural extension workers. Many of them had jobs waiting for them in their local communities when they finished. It seems that a big effort to recruit blacks was made in the South, an area where an overwhelming majority of blacks were the product of the reputedly inferior black public schools, which were not likely to turn out many who would opt for the women's army and score high on the AGCT.

The "eminently qualified person, preferably a Negro recruiter" who was "sent out to colored colleges in order to secure the proper class of applicants" turned out to be fourteen of the thirty-six graduates of the first OCS class. Other black officers were to follow. They were sent to all of the nine service commands—the military areas into which the nation was divided—and the Military District of Washington, D.C. Some of these officers had their own staff of two to four enlisted women. Others worked out of the local recruiting offices. Sometimes, two or more black officers worked the same urban areas as a team. At other times black recruiting officers traveled from place to place through several service commands. Non-black officers at established recruiting centers and the director of the corps and her staff were involved in the recruiting of blacks through public relations activities. Some black civilian leaders, notably Mary McLeod Bethune, and the black press urged blacks to join.[8] (See Appendix 1 for the names and locations of black recruiting officers.)

Officers Dovey M. Johnson and Ruth M. Lucas, who were assigned to the Atlanta office, recounted in some detail their itinerary and their efforts in letters to headquarters in Washington. In November 1942, they reported on their activities in North Carolina. At Charlotte, they talked to groups at Johnson C. Smith College, at two high schools, three elementary schools, the Negro Chamber of Commerce, the Young Women's Christian Association, the larger churches in the city, and at a meeting of the NAACP. They also broadcast a message on a local radio station and received newspaper coverage. At Salisbury, they recruited at Livingstone College, two high schools, one elementary school, a community meeting, a WAAC Day Celebration where exhibits were displayed, and they gave a radio talk and had press coverage. At High Point, they attended a meeting of the Boys and Girls Scout Troop where they gave a fifteen-minute talk. At Spencer, they talked at the Dunbar High School. They recruited at Winston-Salem Teachers College and at two high schools, one elementary school, a community meeting at the Young Women's Christian Association, and twelve churches in the city of Winston-Salem. At Greensboro, they gave a radio talk and addressed groups of students and visitors at Lutheran College, A and T College, and Dudley High School, in addition to making contacts with community groups and getting newspaper coverage.[9]

In their November 22, 1942, letter, Johnson and Lucas sought suggestions and requested any new information about the corps that would aid them in their endeavors. They specifically asked for pictures of "Negro activities" in the WAAC, and they indicated that their work in North Carolina was continuing.[10]

In South Carolina, Johnson and Lucas recruited in Columbia, Orangeburg, and Spartanburg, where they spoke at colleges, high schools, churches, and community gatherings. They sought and received the help of local leaders and groups who were in a position to transmit their message to perspective recruits.[11]

In Florida, Georgia, and elsewhere in the southeast, especially on the campuses of black colleges, in black churches, and black schools, Johnson conducted numerous recruiting drives, some of which extended over several days. In some instances she traveled alone, frequently by bus. Johnson's last recruiting assignment was in Dallas before she was recalled to Fort Des Moines in June 1943. The executive secretary of the Dallas Negro Chamber of Commerce had high praise for her work and regretted her transfer, especially since there would be no replacement.[12]

Harriette B. White told of her recruiting experiences while working out of the Los Angeles Recruiting and Induction District. She agreed with the assessment of black leaders and organizations when she stated that educated blacks were not interested in joining the corps. White also felt that the black press had "retarded" the recruiting program by "forever blasting away at something trivial." She commented on the negative effect that a bulletin of Walter White, executive secretary of the NAACP, would have on recruiting, but she concluded that those blacks who would read it were not going to enroll anyway.[13]

Blanche L. Scott, who was recruiting out of Richmond, stated that she "didn't like recruiting because I'm not a salesman." However, she "went to high schools and colleges trying to get people to join." She felt that the reason for the lack of response to appeals to enroll was "that the public attitude wasn't too favorable about women who joined the Army." Scott added, "People thought that women were going in to be with the men."[14]

Despite her statement that she was "not a salesman," Scott plunged into her assignment with enthusiasm. In Richmond, she spoke of her experiences in the corps and why she had joined and invited others to help the country in its hour of need. She told her audience that "as good Americans, Negro women should want to help win this war as quickly as possible" and that "every woman who enrolls saves that many minutes or perhaps hours of fighting and preserves American lives." She appealed to the patriotism of black women in a similar manner in Portsmouth, Virginia. In Roanoke, she asserted that blacks had to share in "the responsibility of helping to win the war" since this was their country, too. She stated that every woman who joined would release a man for the "fighting front," and this, she said, "helps achieve victory and shortens the war." Scott was very proud when Clara Simon of Richmond, her first recruit, enlisted in the corps and a picture of the recruit appeared in the local press.[15]

Appealing to blacks' sense of patriotism, telling them that their enlistment would release a man for combat duty, and explaining that in so doing they would help shorten the war and save American lives were basically the same themes that other black recruiters used. The others also told potential recruits of the training, job experience, skills, expense-free living, pay, and other benefits that the government provided for those who served. Ethel E. Heywood, who was working out of the Syracuse Recruiting and Induction Station in New York, appeared at forums and radio broadcasts with her non-black colleagues. In Buffalo and Ithaca, she also organized civilian recruiting committees of well-known local blacks who were the lead speakers at the forums and black churches where appeals were made. Heywood's usual closing statement was that the WAC needs black NCOs, the WAC needs black commissioned officers, the WAC needs you—an adaptation of the army's "Uncle Sam Needs You." Like some others, Heywood complained of the time lag between the enrollment of blacks and their shipment to the training center, and of the army's segregated recreational facilities. She regarded these as the two main obstacles in recruiting blacks. The latter obstacle, she said, "has been greatly publicized by the 'Negro Press.' " Despite these obstacles, after just one rally in Buffalo, four of her recruits were enrolled.[16]

Reportedly, black recruits did not "come up to expectations either in quantity or quality" in 1942; although there were plenty of black applicants, as many as 85 percent did not pass the tests. Further, it was stated that only two qualified black applicants—one a typist and the other a clerk—sought to enroll after much effort in the Second Service Command, which included New York City. When standards for all recruits were lowered in the early months of 1943 to boost enlistments, black recruits were singled out for creating "a special problem, in that most of those who met enlistment standards tended to meet only the minimum requirements." Citing test results of a May 1943 sample, 66 percent of the black recruits scored in the lowest AGCT groups of IV and V, compared to 15 percent of the non-blacks. The same sample showed that 43 percent of the non-blacks scored in the two top groups of I and II, while only 6 percent of the blacks ranked that high. Hence, the corps raised its standards in April 1943, apparently to combat "the special problem."[17]

TEN OFFICERS ASSIGNED TO RECRUITING IN 1942

Top, left to right: Mildred Carter, Glendora Moore, Elizabeth C. Hampton, Harriette B. White, Ruth A. Lucas, and Doris M. Norrel. *Bottom, left to right:* Ina M. McFadden, Dovey M. Johnson, Alice M. Jones, and Evelyn F. Green.

After higher standards for enlistment were reimposed in April 1943, most if not all of the black officers were removed from recruiting duties, apparently not only because of the large number of blacks who made low scores on the AGCT but also because of the inability of the War Department to find field commanders willing to accept those blacks who were already in the corps for duty assignments in their commands. When the executive secretary of the Dallas Negro Chamber of Commerce and other black leaders complained about the withdrawal of the officers and requested the corps give serious consideration to the establishment of black recruiting centers staffed by black officers, Harold A. Edlund, an army officer in the office of the director of control division, stated that the "present recruitment of negroes is holding propartionate [sic] to that of whites." He added that "on its merits" he "would not recommend putting negro recruiters back in the field unless the army can use all possible negro" enrollees. Edlund concluded: "However, public policy question involved may dictate that we put them back. I am not in position to be best judge on this point."[18]

It was after Edlund's communication reached Hobby's office, and more than a month after the recruiting officers were removed, that the corps gave an explanation for its action to inquiring black leaders, stating that, because of a shortage of instructors and administrative personnel, the officers were needed at the training centers in order to get black units to field assignments as quickly as possible. The director's office promised the executive director of the Dallas Negro Chamber of Commerce "that everything possible will be done to return such a capable officer as Captain Johnson to recruiting as soon as practicable."[19]

Another reason for the withdrawal of black recruiting officers may have been the perceived effect their presence may have had on non-black recruiting. Referring to complaints reaching headquarters in Washington, the official historian wrote, "It is known that the presence of Negro recruiters had caused situations prejudicial to white recruiting; in Sacramento, California, intelligence operatives reported a serious situation caused by Negro recruiters who

'appeared in public places giving public speeches.' " Moreover, the corps was receiving other types of protests that had
a bearing on recruiting. For example, a man from Roswell,
Minnesota, candidly stated that "putting negroes and whites
in the same barracks is doing more than anything to slow your
recruiting." He added that "even the yankee girls do not like
it."[20]

It is not known how many black officers were subsequently
sent on recruiting duties. At least two were. The corps did
keep its word to L. Virgil Williams of the Dallas Negro
Chamber of Commerce when Dovey M. Johnson was returned for another tour of duty. While in Dallas in late 1943,
she was detailed to assist the Texas campaign of the Third War
Loan Drive. The state chairman of the campaign declared that
she "did a real service and made a fine impression on her
people." Apparently, Johnson became a roving recruiter.
With a staff of two enlisted women—Sergeant Tommy Berry
and Pfc Hazel Washington—she recruited in Warren, Akron,
Cleveland, and Columbus, Ohio, in the latter part of 1943 and
in 1944. Johnson and her team established links with the
black community through the press, churches, social gatherings, social clubs, and civic organizations. Usually, one member of the team served as an advance person to establish
contact with the local groups, and these groups in turn
provided a forum for the team's activities.[21]

In Columbus, the Youth Department of the Urban League
sponsored one of Johnson's recruiting drives. Its director,
Edwina T. Glascer, felt that the participation of Harriet M.
West, then the highest-ranking black officer, would heighten
local interest in the corps and attract a larger audience.
Glascer's first request for West, who was stationed at headquarters in Washington, went unanswered. Her second request, dated December 29, 1943, was not acknowledged until
January 12, 1944, and it was not until the first week of the
following month that West made an appearance. Although
the recruiting campaign in Columbus was a success, and both
Johnson and West were commended for their outstanding
performances by both Glascer and Hobby, it seems that the
slowness of the WAC in responding to Glascer's request

indicated something less than enthusiasm for the project—
and this at a time when the corps, its civilian committees, and
its recruiters were making a big pitch for enrollees.[22]

Ruth L. Freeman and her team of sergeants Ruth Parker
and Bennie Evans were recruiting in Chicago and other
locations in the Sixth Service Command. In addition to the
usual techniques used by others, Freeman sought out enter-
tainers and celebrities who happened to be in the city, local
artists and civic leaders, and black folk heroes to share the
spotlight with her and her team as they appealed for volun-
teers to join the corps. In April 1945, when it was feared that
Freeman's operation was going to be cut back, a leader of a
local black organization sought the help of the NAACP to
save it. He bemoaned the fact that Freeman's group were the
only black recruiters in the entire Sixth Service Command
while two hundred white recruiters were on the job and
would probably remain on the job.[23]

Persistent stories, innuendoes, and rumors about women
becoming social companions for the servicemen had a negative effect on recruiting both black and non-black women.
The "prostitution thing," as it was called, seems to have had
more of an effect on blacks, possibly because of their social
status. Dovey M. Johnson stated that she found the "prostitution thing" to have been a greater deterrent to recruiting than
the policy of enforced segregation. She said that she was
constantly questioned about the intention of the army in
respect to the use of women, especially black women.[24]
Blanche L. Scott also regarded this as an important concern.

A serious incident occurred in the summer of 1944 at
Camp Forrest (Tennessee) and was of special concern to
blacks. Non-black soldiers on the post allegedly threatened to
invade the barracks of the black WACs and to rape them. One
report from an enlisted woman on the scene stated that the
soldiers actually broke into the barracks. At any rate, the
alleged threats were picked up by some black soldiers on post,
and talk that these two groups of soldiers might square off
reached post headquarters. The incident was considered
serious enough to warrant the attention of the Inspector
General's office at headquarters in Washington. The WAC
area at the camp was declared off-limits to non-black soldiers

and placed under guard. An account of this incident appeared in the August 12, 1944, issue of the *Amsterdam Star News.*[25] News of this nature undoubtedly exacerbated the concern of the black community and haunted recruiters, both black and non-black.

In summing up Colonel Oveta Culp Hobby's stewardship as director of the corps on the eve of her retirement, the *Chicago Defender,* a black newspaper, in an article in its July 21, 1945, issue, noted that "at one stage of the game she completely withdrew Negro recruiting officers from the field complaining that the type of recruit they were bringing in was decidedly inferior." The article stated that when Colonel Hobby was asked whether the caliber of Negro recruits improved under the selective process of white officers, she quickly replied yes. The account stated further that when the director was pressed on whether the improved quality of the recruits was due to the higher standards that were imposed, and hence there was no basis for comparison, the director did not respond. Rather, the article concluded, she excused herself from the conference with the black leaders on the plea that she had another appointment.

In late 1944, however, an increasing number of sick and wounded men from the European and Pacific theaters were being returned to the States for treatment. To care for these men, the War Department's Surgeon General's Office had expanded its facilities and opened new installations. There was a need for more WACs trained as medical and surgical technicians and laboratory aides to staff these facilities, so educational requirements were lowered, the enlistment age limit was raised to forty-nine years again, and potential recruits were promised that they would be assigned to the hospitals for which they were recruited. The War Department made two urgent appeals for recruits, and blacks were expected to volunteer. The *Oklahoma Eagle* and some other black newspapers carried the news item in their February 1945 issues. The *Eagle* reported that "Gardiner General Hospital, one of the Army's largest general hospitals," sought black WACs "as nurses' assistants."[26] This was the last big drive for black recruits.

A confidential policy statement was circulated to each

service command during the early life of the organization informing the commands that "every effort will be made through intensive recruiting to obtain the class of colored women desired, in order that there may be no lowering of standards in order to meet ratio requirements." The War Department also sent periodic notices to each service command reminding it that "no more than 10%" of its recruits should be black. Sometimes these notices contained the precise figures for non-black and black recruits expected from a designated service command.[27] The service commands, therefore, knew that they did not have to take all of the blacks who applied—not even all of these who met the enlistment requirements.

Of those blacks who did apply, 50 percent were rejected because of low aptitude test scores and for administrative reasons resulting, in the main, from personal interviews, compared to 22 percent of the non-blacks. From 1942 to June 1943, about 40 percent of all blacks were disqualified for medical or health reasons, compared to 25 percent of all non-blacks. In the first four months of 1944, 529 blacks were enrolled, an average of 138 per month. In the last four months of 1944, black enrollment averaged 130 per month, with the December 1944 enrollment standing at 100. As a result of test scores of those applying in late 1944, it was estimated that black enrollment thereafter would average 57 per month. During the first week of April 1945, when the war in Europe was still in progress, 482 non-blacks were accepted in the corps, compared to 4 blacks. During the entire period of the war, a total of about 6,500 blacks enrolled in the corps, representing about 4.3 percent of the total number of women admitted to the corps.[28]

Once accepted, some blacks waited longer than the customary ten days or two weeks before being called to active duty. The service commands had instructions as early as November 1942 to retain blacks on an inactive duty status "until a sufficient number has been enrolled to facilitate their being called in groups of 50 or more." As of April 30, 1943, 645 blacks were on inactive duty awaiting orders to move to the training centers. Harriette B. White, a black recruiting officer in Los Angeles, had wondered earlier why they "were slow moving Negro enrollees after enlistment." She noted that some women whom she had recruited had been on inactive duty for over a month. She complained that delays in calling them up had a negative effect on recruiting.[29]

The WAC never did attain the "10.6 percent of its strength in Negro recruits" that it "was directed to accept," a number roughly equal to the proportion of blacks in the population of the United States. The closest the corps ever came to this quota was when it enrolled 40 blacks in the first OCS class of about 440.[30] From that point, the number of blacks never reached 6 percent of the strength of the corps.

The official records of the army show that the proportion of black women in the service at the end of December 1942 was 1.7 percent, or 220 out of a total of 12,767. Six months later—June 30, 1943—the 3,161 blacks represented 5.2 percent of the strength of the corps. When 3,012 blacks were in the WAC at the end of September 1943, they represented 5.9 percent of the number of women in the organization. Except for the first month or so of the corps existence, this 5.9 percent was the highest proportion of blacks in the organization during World War II, and this percentage was achieved, significantly, when the Women's Army Auxiliary Corps became the Women's Army Corps, an integral part of the Army of the United States, and when 343 officers and 14,607 enlisted women did not reenlist. When black enrollment peaked at 4,040 at the end of December 1944, it was only 4.5 percent of the total strength of the corps. In March 1945, when the war was still being fought on all fronts, black enrollment stood at 3,902, or 4.1 percent of the total number of women in the service. In April 1945, when the WAC attained its top strength of 99,288 women, black enrollment was about 3,900, or 3.9 percent of the total. By the end of 1945, only 1,690 of the 43,813 WACs were black[31] (See Appendix 2 for the number and percentage of blacks in the corps at specific times.)

Separating the number of officers from the official data, the percentage of blacks among them is much less. The 59 black officers reported in the corps in December 1942 consisted of 3.8 percent of the total officer strength of 1,545. This percentage represented the highest proportion of black

42   **Blacks in the Women's Army Corps**

officers in the corps for the rest of the period under study. Of the 5,856 officers in the service in December 1943, the 103 blacks among them represented 1.75 percent of the total. The highest number of black officers reported in the WAC at any one time was 121 in September 1944, and they represented 2.04 percent of the 5,930 officers on active duty, the largest number of officers on active duty at any one time. Thereafter, both the number of officers and the number of blacks among them declined—proportionally at first, but more precipitously for blacks near the end of the period. In March 1945, two months before V-E Day, 115 black officers were in the corps. In December 1945, the 80 blacks made up 1.8 percent of the officer corps. By the end of 1946, only 9, or .75 percent, of the 1,189 officers were black. Moreover, none of the 60 female warrant officers were black.[32] (See Appendix 2.)

But there is reason to question the reported data on the number of black officers in the corps. As noted previously, 36 finished with the first OCS class and were commissioned on August 29, 1942. The next blacks to enter OCS were in the eleventh class, and the members of this class were not commissioned until January 9, 1943. (For the number of blacks, their OCS classes, and the dates of commissioning, see Appendix 3.) Hence, there could not have been 59 black officers in the corps as of December 31, 1942, as indicated in Appendix 2. The figure of 65 black officers shown to have been in the corps in March 1943 is wrong since it is evidently calculated on an incorrect base number of 59. Data on black officers for the subsequent stated periods in Appendix 2 may suffer from the same flaw. Most if not all of the data in Appendix 2 apparently were extracted from the monthly "Strength of the Army" reports which routinely carried a notice requesting recipients to provide correct information for errors therein.[33]

The information in Appendix 3 supposedly is based on documents and papers from the Fort Des Moines records. The 41 blacks shown to have been in the first OCS class may have been the number of blacks actually selected for this class. Papers in the Bethune Archives contain the names of 41 women who presumably were chosen for this class, and 41 probably started with the class. Further, the photograph released to the press in connection with the commissioning of the first class, shows the likenesses, names, and hometowns of 39 black women and their non-black male cadre. This picture may have been the source for listing incorrectly 39 blacks as having been commissioned with the first class. There were instances, of course, where the number of blacks in a class picture actually reflected the number who were commissioned, as can be observed from the picture of the thirty-fifth OCS class.

It also appears that the information in Appendix 3 on the eleventh and twelfth classes is transposed, and some is incorrect. Headquarters in Washington issued a press release on January 9, 1943, the very day of an "impressive ceremony," announcing that "seven outstanding" black women had "graduated from the eleventh Officer Candidate School at Fort Des Moines." The names of the seven individuals along with a brief biographical sketch of each one were provided to the press. Actually, nine (not seven) blacks were commissioned on January 9, 1943. Although Appendix 3 shows that six blacks were commissioned with the forty-second class, only four blacks appear on the special orders commissioning the eighty members of this class at Fort Oglethorpe on October 16, 1943.[34]

Indeed, no definitive numbers emerge on how many black officers were in the corps at stated periods or how many were commissioned during World War II. For example, in a memorandum dated February 12, 1943, Director Hobby informed Truman K. Gibson, Jr., the acting civilian aide to the secretary of war, that there were forty-five black officers at that time. About a month later, on April 13, 1943, Director Hobby was told that at the end of each of the first three months of 1943 there were 45, 56, and 58 black officers, respectively. Then, in August 1943, when the editor of the *Negro Handbook* sought information about blacks in the corps, she was told that the WAC did not keep figures by race. Yet she was informed that there were eight black captains, thirty first lieutenants, and seventy-one second lieutenants. These numbers added up to 109 black officers.[35]

The table below provides a basis for reviewing these data on the number of black officers.

Above: Official photograph of first graduating class with WAAC members from Officer Candidate School.

Opposite: Thirty-fifth Officer Candidate School class.

Data from:

	Appendix 2	Appendix 3	WAC Head-quarters
December 31, 1942	59	39	NA
January 31, 1943	NA	50	45
February 12, 1943	NA	51	45
February 28, 1943	NA	52	56
March 31, 1943	65	54	58
June 30, 1943	105	98	NA
August 7, 1943	NA	107	109
September 30, 1943	105	111	NA

Appendix 3 does not purport to show how many blacks were in the corps at stated periods, but rather how many were commissioned and when they were commissioned. Yet it appears at least in regard to the first, eleventh, twelfth, and forty-second classes that the data in Appendix 3 are incorrect. It appears that the figures in Appendix 2 on the number of black officers in the corps for December 1942, March 1943, and June 1943 are overstated, as are the data from WAC Headquarters for February 28, 1943; March 31, 1943; and August 7, 1943. (See Appendix 4 for the names, hometowns and army serial numbers of the black officers in the first class and those in subsequent classes.)

It is noteworthy that, although 343 officers did not reenlist when the WAAC converted to the WAC on September 1, 1943, the table above seems to indicate that no more than 4 of them could have been black. However, the overall attrition rate for blacks was very high. It was estimated that 6,500 blacks enrolled in the corps during the period under study. The data in Appendix 2 indicate that no more than 4,040 of them were in the service at any one time. The attrition rate, therefore, exceeded 35 percent, a very significant decrease. An examination of the data in Appendix 2 shows that black enrollment increased measurably from December 1942 to June 1943, then showed a decline for September 1943 and December 1943. This decline seems to reflect two trends: blacks already in the service were being discharged, and fewer blacks were entering the service. The attrition for those four months—from September to December 1943—was much higher than for any other period until the end of the war with Japan. The beginning of this decline coincided with the removal of black officers from recruiting duties and occurred while the corps was vigorously recruiting and while enrollment in the WAC was increasing significantly. Indeed, the National Civilian Advisory Committee was apprised of the decline in black recruits at a meeting in February 1945.[36]

Concern about how they would be used and treated, the policy of segregation, and the state of race relations in the nation led to a reluctance on the part of a large number of blacks (including most of the better-qualified ones) to join the volunteer corps. The removal of black officers from recruiting, the raising of entrance standards, and, to a lesser degree, the retention of a significant number of black women on inactive status too long prevented or discouraged some who might have wanted to join from enrolling. During their tours of duty, however, the black recruiting officers evidently did a fantastic job of inducing a large number of women to apply even though many of them were denied enrollment. Some of the high attrition rate among those who did enroll was due more to the practice of segregation than to the policy of segregation.

3. SEGREGATION

Those entering the corps knew that they were going to be segregated. The director of the corps in her initial press conference stated publicly that the WAAC would follow existing army policy. About ten days later—on May 27, 1942—in response to numerous letters and inquiries, the army's adjutant general's office expanded on and formalized the War Department policy. The statement read that the corps would be governed by the army model but "there shall be no discrimination because of race, creed or national origin." Further, in a confidential statement circulated within the military, it was stipulated that

> on posts where these [black] companies are stationed, it should be fundamental that their reception and treatment should be an exemplication [*sic*] of the rights and privileges accorded officers and soldiers of the United States Army. . . . There will be no discrimination in the type of duties to which Negro women in the WAAC may be assigned.[1]

The NAACP, among other organizations, had lobbied hard for the inclusion of a non-discrimination clause in the enabling act. Specifically, the NAACP wanted Congress to write into the law authorizing the corps a clause stating that there would be no discrimination in enrollment, assignments, ratings, promotions, or opportunities for the advancement of blacks.[2] The adjutant general's statement was circulated after the corps was operational, perhaps because not very many of the better-qualified blacks were applying for entry. In any event, it was circulated among individuals in an organization which had a long history of discriminating against blacks.

For some of those who entered, segregation and discrimination began before they reached the training centers. Some recruits who arrived in Chicago at night on their way to Fort Des Moines were separated by race at the train station. The non-blacks were escorted away by army personnel, and blacks were told to make their way to a designated rooming house. They had to locate their overnight quarters on their own in a strange city, sometimes in the dark of the night. The next day these black recruits made their way back to the railroad station, again on their own, while the non-blacks returned escorted by army personnel.[3]

Horace R. Cayton, a black Chicago businessman, had a contract with the army to provide overnight lodging for black inductees who had train layovers en route to Fort Des Moines. Cayton was not satisfied with the way the women were sent to him or with the inconvenience he suffered. He complained that the women were "sent any time" in the night to his place. He stated that they were sent "without supervision and protection." He related that sometimes he had no beds for them and had to scurry about to find accommodations. He mentioned that non-blacks were taken to "Loop hotels" under escort.[4]

Some three weeks later, on July 26, 1944, Jeanetta Welch Brown, then executive secretary of the National Council of Negro Women, wrote to Colonel Hobby criticizing the army's treatment of blacks arriving in Chicago who were sent "late at night without chaperones or other guides" to lodging places. The whites, she wrote, "are taken to hotels and supervised." Brown wanted the army to remedy the situation. Cayton had already returned his contract to the army with the explanation that the arrangement had not turned out very satisfactory either for the black women or for his business.[5]

Segregation began for most blacks as soon as they entered the training centers in civilian clothes. As they exited from the army vehicles that had transported them from the depot, they were directed to a segregated formation or unit or barracks. This practice started with the very first group to enter the WAAC as officer candidates when the non-black army officer greeted them by yelling: "Negroes on one side! White girls on the other."

These forty experienced an assortment of denigrating

situations which the army categorized collectively as segregation. They were housed separately as a company, off officers' row and around the corner from their classmates. They marched as a single unit apart from the larger companies; they filed into classrooms and took seats in a special section set apart for them; and they entered the mess hall as a unit and confronted reserved tables with signs marked Colored.[6]

Those "neat little signs" on the mess tables, observed one of the black OCS members, were so unnecessary and so humiliating that the women asked the post commandant why they were there. The women reasoned with the commandant that since they entered the mess hall in single file from a marching formation, they would as a matter of course have been seated together. The commandant disclaimed any knowledge of the existence of the signs, and shortly thereafter, they disappeared from the tables. The black officer said that the removal of the signs did not change anything. They were given orders to sit at those tables, and the whites were under orders not to sit there.[7] The officer remarked that nobody needed those signs, that they were an overkill. The blacks did not need to be reminded who they were, and others could see who they were.[8]

There was more. Blacks were banned from the whites-only service club; they were expected to use instead a small recreation room in the rear of their barracks. It was not until after they had completed OCS that a newly constructed service club was ready for blacks. By that time it was too late for them, since service clubs were social and recreational centers for enlisted personnel. And the officers club, which was the social and recreational center for commissioned officers, was off-limits to blacks. The swimming pool was also off-limits to them, except for one hour on Friday evenings; the non-blacks had orders not to use the pool during that hour. Immediately after the blacks used the pool, the water was cleansed and purified.[9]

The director of the corps, when questioned about the situation confronted by the blacks in the first OCS class, found nothing unusual about the arrangements. Everything, she stated, was scheduled by companies. A service club for blacks, she told her questioners, was under construction, as was a new service club for non-blacks. However, both she and her staff disclaimed any knowledge of the signs on the mess hall tables and the "reserved seats" in the classrooms. Besides, a member of Hobby's staff said that Mary McLeod Bethune had described the operation as "democracy in action" and had advised the black women not to complain.[10]

Bethune, who was for all practical purposes the surrogate mother of the black WACs and one of twenty-three prominent female members of the National Civilian Advisory Committee which met regularly to advise the director of the WAC and her staff, was then being used as a fall guy. In a memorandum dated June 1, 1942, Bethune had indeed endorsed the WAAC and urged black women to join. But she had made it very clear that her endorsement was not of the policy of segregation, which she noted, was another battle that had to be fought and won. Later, when Bethune visited Fort Des Moines shortly after the first OCS class had arrived, she greeted the entire group of blacks, told them that they represented the blacks of America, and said: "Here at Ft. Des Moines we have democracy in action. We are seeking equal participation. We are not going to be agitators." The National Council of Negro Women, of which Bethune was a founding member and influential member, in an early report to the War Department explicitly stated that the council was "working towards the goal of full integration" of blacks in the corps. The council also urged the army to utilize its black members "within the framework of democracy."[11]

The army, however, saw fit to interpret Bethune's remarks to the women to mean that she had condoned segregation and had advised the women not to complain. When black leaders and the press complained about the segregation and discrimination in the corps, the army told them what Bethune had said. Thus, thrown on the defensive, Bethune had to refute publicly the views attributed to her by the military. She acknowledged making the statements about "democracy in action" and "not being agitators," but she said that she had told the corps and the army that she wanted equal participation, and that from the beginning (even before the WAAC became operational) both she and the National Council of

Negro Women had made it clear to the military that they could not condone segregation.[12]

While Bethune was setting the record straight on her opposition to segregation, the army for its part was trying to find out who among the black OCS students had talked to the press and who among the non-black male army personnel had made the racist remarks which the press had reported. During the course of this inquiry, the commanding officer of the black OCS unit told his troops that the *Pittsburgh Courier*, whose executive editor had complained to Director Hobby, was "a trouble maker" and "not worth the paper it is printed on." One of the black OCS students, later reportedly, identified as Harriet M. West, agreed with the substance of her commanding officer's remarks about the black newspaper.[13]

Another black newspaper official, Charles F. Howard, was accused of trying to persuade black officer candidates to talk about unjust treatment and discrimination. Howard was the owner of the *Iowa Observer*, a weekly newspaper, and of the Howard News Syndicate, which (according to Fort Des Moines sources) was in the business of sending out articles and pictures about WAACs to black newspapers. Howard's son was the editor of the paper, and Howard Sr. maintained a law office in Des Moines and was reported to have been twice disbarred ten years previously. He was regarded by Fort Des Moines authorities as a nuisance because he was attempting "to incite race prejudice."[14]

It was probably because of the onslaught of attention and criticism by the black press, leaders, and organizations that Harriet M. West was assigned shortly after having been commissioned to the director's staff at the War Department as "advisor on Negro affairs." West's first assignment at headquarters was in the office of inspection and control, where she monitored recruiting irregularities. However, by September 1943 she was reassigned to the adjutant general's office, where she was supervisor of the casualty branch, which sent out notifications to the next of kin of the dead and wounded. Prior to entering the service, West had been an assistant to Bethune, then the Director of Negro Affairs in the National Youth Administration.[15] West's assignment at the policy-making level was apparently an attempt to take the wind out of some of the criticism, but it continued.

Walter White, the executive secretary of the NAACP, did not like what he saw at Fort Des Moines and at the OCS school in particular. He addressed a joint letter to Secretary of War Henry L. Stimson and Director Hobby in which he lamented all of the segregation and discrimination that he observed at the fort and in the OCS there. He recalled his visit to Fort Sill (Oklahoma), where there was no segregation and an apparent acceptance of black officer candidates by the white students. White wanted to know why the army segregated and discriminated against black women at the OCS at Fort Des Moines.[16]

In segregating the first class at Fort Des Moines, the military was not adhering to "the same liberal policy with respect to Negroes that exists in the Army." Neither at the military academy at West Point nor at any of its officer candidate schools did the army separate its students as completely as it did the black and non-black at Fort Des Moines. The reason for this departure from its "liberal policy" was the number of blacks in the class: forty in a class of four hundred, compared with the usual West Point and OCS classes of a mere handful or fewer blacks.[17]

Confronted with complaints from black organizations and leaders and from some of the black officer candidates in the first class, in early November 1942, at a time when no blacks were in attendance at OCS, an army officer recommended "that Officer Candidate School should not be segregated in the future since there will, no doubt, be enough for a full platoon of colored" students. Two weeks later, Colonel Hobby, responding to charges of segregation in the corps, issued a statement to the press, which read in part:

> The Women's Army Auxiliary is a young and growing organization. Its regulations change to meet changing needs but in general policy the corps must follow policies of the War Department of which it is a part.
>
> The application of the army's policy in relation to mingling of white and colored personnel is a variable one determined by the size of the group concerned.

At officers' candidate training schools in the army, colored candidates constitute a separate unit if there are a sufficient number; otherwise, they are absorbed into the white units. Exactly the same is true at the WAAC training center at Fort Des Moines. The initial group of colored officer candidates was sufficiently large to form an entire platoon. At the present moment among the first officer candidates to be chosen from the auxiliary there are ten colored candidates and they being a small group have been absorbed into the training company.

They all live in the same barracks and share the same mess.[18]

About the same time, Walter White and William Hastie, civilian aides to the secretary of war, in a conference at the Pentagon with army Colonel J. Noel Macy of the WAAC Group and WAAC staff officers Helen Woods and Harriet M. West, received assurances that "the segregation of colored WAAC officers had been abolished" and that "the ten auxiliaries who had been chosen for officer candidate school would not be segregated." White had tried but failed to obtain a promise that OCS would not be re-segregated in the event there would be "a sufficient number of [black] officer candidates to form a company." White then requested the corps to establish "a rule to govern any contingency of this sort" so that there would have been conformity with the training of male officers.[19]

In all of the OCS classes except the first, there were either no blacks or fewer than 11, with the exceptions of the twenty-eighth (which had 15 in a group of 149) and the thirty-first (which had 14 in a group of 264). The eleventh class, which began its training on November 16, 1942, was both the second class to admit blacks and the second class to accept students from the ranks of enlisted women or from the "auxiliary." This was the class that Director Hobby had stated was "absorbed into the training company" and was in session when White and Hastie were told that "segregation of colored WAAC officers had been abolished." However, the blacks in this class were organized as a separate squad and quartered in a separate squad room. The twelfth class, which began on

November 30, 1943, and had fewer black students evidently, was the first class to be desegregated.[20]

Noteworthy in this regard is the contrasting ethnic composition of the photographs showing blacks in the first class and those in the thirty-fifth class. After the first class, blacks averaged a little over four students per class in the thirty other classes to which they were admitted. Hence, the ethnic composition of the thirty-fifth class may be regarded as a typical WAAC/WAC OCS class for these thirty classes. Twenty-nine of the sixty OCS classes—almost one-half of them—had no black students (see Appendix 3).

An incident at the Savery Hotel in the city of Des Moines where WAACs were stationed was one of the factors that led the War Department to dispatch a staff officer to Fort Des Moines for an on-the-spot investigation of race relations. An officer on location at the Savery Hotel had ordered some black officers in the mess to move their trays and to sit at a table designated for blacks. The officer used the term "darky" in speaking to the black officers. Ten black officers sent a telegram to Mary McLeod Bethune complaining of the "unnecessary prejudice in the dining hall at the Savery Hotel" and stating that conditions were becoming intolerable on the post. The telegram also noted that officials at Fort Des Moines had told some of the black officers that Harriet M. West and Bethune had approved of the situation there.[21]

Prior to the arrival of the staff officer from the War Department, Colonel Morgan, then acting post commandant, singled out Dovey M. Johnson and Irma J. Cayton as the instigators of the group action. He confronted these two officers, called them "agitators," charged them with "treason," and asked for their resignations. Colonel Morgan's scare tactics did not work; the officers knew the definition of "treason" and knew that what Colonel Morgan was talking about was not it. Irma J. Cayton did, however, offer to submit a letter of resignation on the condition that she could explain fully in it the incident, including Morgan's badgering. Morgan refused this offer and insisted on a simple letter of resignation, which he did not get.[22] It appears to have been common practice in the army to seek out those who went outside of military channels with their problems and attempt to nail them for some infraction of the Articles of War or army regulations.

Shortly after this session with Morgan, the staff officer from the War Department arrived on the post. He made a thorough investigation of the conditions there and made several recommendations designed to improve race relations. Among them was one to permit officers to sit where they desired in the mess hall, recalling the incident in the Savery Hotel that had sparked the telegram. He likewise tried and failed to identify those responsible for contacting Bethune.[23]

The women in the black band had an unpleasant experience. The band got started when a few blacks with skills or training in musical instruments expressed a desire to join the already established post band, and were turned down. When they persisted in their efforts, it was suggested that they organize their own band. They did just that and were recognized as a functional unit by post headquarters. Most of the members of this thirty-five-piece unit had no previous band experience, about one-fifth of them had very limited training or experience in instrumental music or choral music or church choir singing, and only three had played in bands previously. What all of them had was a tremendous desire to play in a WAC band and a capacity to learn. The women had worked hard to learn the intricacies of band playing and to improve their skills. They had taken off-duty courses in music at Drake University in Des Moines. They had practiced diligently and had a great deal of pride in their work. They had arrived at a point where they were making good music together and were getting "a little respect." They had held a number of concerts on and off the post, had participated in a Memorial Day parade in downtown Des Moines on May 30, 1944, and had played at the Central Young Women's Christian Association in Des Moines in June 1944. And they had been rewarded with technical ratings for their accomplishments.[24]

Then the War Department sent out a memorandum stating that there were too many bands on some posts and that personnel from the excess bands were to be released for essential duties. Hence, after nine months in existence—from about August 1943 to about June 1944—the black band was deactivated. The women again sought permission to join the other band on the post and were rejected. Shortly thereafter, they lost the technical ratings they had worked so hard to earn.[25]

When the news of the band's plight reached the public, critics took the army to task for disbanding the unit. Walter White complained to Stimson about the deactivation and suggested that the women be permitted to join the other band on the post. This suggestion was ignored. White was told that the War Department had never authorized the band and that therefore the band should never have existed.[26]

Letters of protest and concern about the deactivation of the band came from a number of individuals and organizations, including Jeanette Welch Brown of the National Council of Negro Women, Ike Small of the Racial Justice Committee of the Des Moines Interracial Commission, the president of Knoxville (Tennessee) College, Herbert T. Miller of the Carlton Avenue Branch of the Brooklyn and Queens Young Men's Christian Association, and Harry W. Gray of Local 208 of the Musicians' Protective Union. The War Department responded to these letters in basically the same manner that it responded to Walter White's letter: personnel was needed for essential duties, and it had never authorized the band. Some of these letters entreated the army and the corps to open the ranks of the official post band to blacks. These entreaties were also ignored. The army and the corps had decided early to not allow themselves to be "forced to make decisions relative to racial matters which the government and/or the citizens should have made long ago." Accordingly, the director of the corps would step aside, and the army policy would prevail in matters of this nature.[27] Colonel Frank U. McCoskrie, the commandant at Fort Des Moines, explained to those asking him about WAC Band No. 2, as it was called, that "there cannot be two bands kept [on] this post," and that in effect his hands were tied.[28] Bethune made several inquiries about the band to the staff of the director of the corps. Then, on August 14, 1944, she wrote directly to Colonel Hobby. She wanted the women to be allowed to join the established band or have the black band reactivated.[29]

Assistant Secretary of War John J. McCloy, after reading a copy of a letter to President Roosevelt asking him to save the "only black WAC band in the United States" and other correspondence on the band, concluded that "the band has become somewhat of a symbol [of discrimination] to the colored people and there is considerable feeling and pressure for its continuance." He noted that there were four authorized non-black WAC bands and recommended that it was "not advisable to disband" the black unit.[30]

In the meantime, Colonel McCoskrie recognized that the deactivation of the band could cause a morale problem among blacks on the post. He had already noted that the black band members were dispirited. He also knew that others on the post wanted to know why at least some of the black band members could not be permitted to join the authorized band if there could be only one band. Hence, he sent a letter through channels to the War Department recommending that the band be retained. He believed, he wrote, that the morale benefits of retaining the band would outweigh the benefits which might have issued from the transfer and reassignment of the band's personnel at that time.[31]

The War Department approved McCoskrie's recommendation, and stated that it had previously taken the position that "it was in the interest of furtherance of the war effort," that, in effect, the need for personnel in other urgent areas of endeavor "did not justify so many Army bands." So, before Bethune's letter reached Colonel Hobby's desk, she received a letter dated August 10, 1944, informing her that the black band would be reactivated.[32]

The band was reassembled and officially designated the 404th Army Service Forces Band, but it had to wait for the replacement of its instruments before resuming its activities. Lieutenant Ernestine L. Woods, who had studied music at Howard University in Washington, D.C., became its commanding officer. Neither Lieutenant Thelma B. Brown nor Lieutenant Alice M. McAlpine, the previous commanding officers of the black band, nor Ernestine L. Woods had had any prior experience in directing bands. All three had had college training in music and at least one had taught music at the college level. Yet everyone at Fort Des Moines declared

that "it had more rhythm and could be drilled to more easily than the 400th Army Service Forces Band," the non-black band on the post. It was the only all-black band in the corps, and before the end of the war it was redesignated the 404th Army Band and received its first non-black commanding officer.[33]

Although the corps permitted eighty of the Aircraft Warning Service's employees to enter the first WAAC OCS class, the service seemed unwilling to accept the assignment of blacks at its installations. When the corps made the request, the service refused to accept blacks regardless of the length of their tour of duty. The reason given at that time was that the service "can not mix the races" and that there would not be enough blacks for a separate unit. After being apprised that the War Department policy was "to give qualified Negro women the same opportunity" accorded to non-blacks, and after two days of negotiations or "conferences," the commanding general of the First Fighter Command proposed forming a black unit and sending it to Thomasville, Georgia. The commandant at Fort Des Moines, in accord with the sentiment of the director of the corps, countered with the proposal of forming two units: one to be stationed in the North and one to be stationed in the South.[34]

Thinking that it had an understanding with the Aircraft Warning Service, the corps prepared to put together a black company and to move it to the field on March 29, 1943. This unit was to be assigned to the Fifteenth WAAC Filter, Aircraft Warning Service, at Syracuse, New York, and at the same time the non-black unit at Syracuse was to be moved to Albany, New York. Then, apparently, the agreement that the corps thought it had fell through, and all WAAC Aircraft Warning Service companies were disbanded. The service commands (the military districts into which the nation was divided) were given permission to use the personnel of these companies to fill their vacancies.[35]

Some blacks took the occasion of the impending conversion of the organization from the WAAC to the WAC to resign because of racial discrimination. Six women at Camp Breckenridge (Kentucky), for example, left the service after protesting about their discriminatory job assignments. They were members of a company trained at Fort Des Moines and sent to Camp Breckenridge to work in army supply. Reportedly, they were given jobs stacking beds and scrubbing floors in a warehouse. They protested these job assignments and were "rewarded" by being assigned to washing walls in a laundry, whereupon they went on strike. On July 1, 1943, they were allowed to resign.[36] These women were all from the North—one from New Jersey and five from New York. They said that most of the women in their unit were from the Southern states and that these women were wary about protesting. The War Department later acknowledged that these six women had not been given proper assignments.[37]

Four WACs working as orderlies at Lovell General Hospital at Fort Devens (Massachusetts) did not have the option of resigning when they became victims of job discrimination. The predicament that they found themselves in did not occur until after the corps became an integral part of the Army of the United States. Their case attracted national attention. The four—privates Alice Young, Anna C. Morrison, Johnnie Murphy, Mary E. Green—were members of a black company assigned to Lovell General Hospital. Some of the members of this unit had had experience in hospital work. Private Young had spent a year in an accredited nurses' training program before enrolling in the WAC in 1944. After basic training at Fort Des Moines, Young, among others, was sent to the field.[38] The incident involving these four and other members of their unit began when Colonel Walter H. Crandall, the commandant of Lovell General Hospital, spotted Young teaching another WAC how to take a temperature. The colonel wanted to know what Young was doing, and Young's supervising nurse explained that Young was a medical technician and was taking temperatures. The colonel then reportedly declared: "I don't want any black WACs as medical technicians around this hospital. I want them to scrub and do the dirty work." The colonel is said to have made it demonstrably clear to the black WACs that "they are here to mop, [wash] walls and do all the dirty work." When Young requested an assignment to the motor pool, the colonel is said to have asserted, "They want no black WACs working at the motor pool."[39]

All of the black WACs at one time or another—some on more than one occasion—had been told the stated policy of the War Department that "there will be no discrimination in the type of duties to which Negro women in the WAC may be assigned." At Lovell General Hospital at that time, the black WACs were assigned as orderlies and the non-black WACs were assigned as technicians. So when Private Young and those who were with her revealed the colonel's remarks to the other members of their unit, a number of them decided not to report for duty. They in effect staged a strike,[40] taking the War Department at its word and inviting it to correct a wrong. But the army officials at Fort Devens and those in charge up through the First Service Command, in which Fort Devens was located, prepared to throw the book at them.

To break the strike, a ranking non-black WAC officer, some army officers, and then the commanding general of the First Service Command, Major General Sherman Miles, ordered the women to return to duty under the authority of the Sixty-fourth Article of War, prohibiting the willful disobeying of a lawful command or order of their superior officers. Although some black WAC officers, including the unit's commanding officer, were on the post at Fort Devens at that time, apparently none stepped forward or was asked to step forward "to read the riot act" to the women, nor did it appear that their views on the discriminatory nature of the job assignments were clearly known to the women or to the post authorities. After the women received the ominous word from General Miles, all except four complied with the order to return to duty. These four—privates Young, Green, Murphy, and Morrison—were ordered to stand trial before a general court-martial for their refusal to obey the orders of superior officers.[41]

The nine-member court consisted of two non-black WAC officers, two black army officers, and five other army officers. Lieutenant Tenola T. Stoney, the commanding officer of the black company, told the court that she heard Colonel Crandall make the remark about not wanting blacks working in the motor pool. The colonel himself later attributed that remark to the officer in charge of the motor pool. The four WACs on trial told the court that blacks were assigned as orderlies while non-blacks worked as technicians. They recounted in graphic detail their encounter with Colonel Crandall and his telling them that he wanted no blacks as medical technicians but only to "do the dirty work" of scrubbing, mopping, and washing walls. The four were represented by Julian D. Rainey, A Boston attorney affiliated with the National Association for the Advancement of Colored People.[42]

The trial lasted two days, and it took the court less than two hours to reach a verdict of guilty; the women actually did willfully disobey orders of superior officers, and that was the charge. They were on trial; Colonel Crandall, whose defiance of the War Department's policy got the four women in their predicament, was not. The four were sentenced to one year at hard labor and dishonorable discharge from the service. When the verdict was read, one of the WACs, emotionally drained, broke down completely and had to be assisted from the courtroom.[43]

The case was sent up for review to headquarters of the First Service Command, to General Miles, the man who invoked the reading of Article Sixty-four of the Articles of War and hence set in motion the court-martial. According to established procedure, headquarters of the First Service Command was the next step in the chain of command, but in this instance General Miles was in reality the grand jury, the prosecutor, and the review judge. Black leaders were certain that the sentence was unduly harsh in view of the circumstances surrounding the incident. Three New York congressmen asked the War Department to investigate the case. Other individuals asked the War Department to remove Colonel Crandall.[44]

The War Department reversed the verdict in the case and restored the women to duty, but it left Colonel Crandall in place. This increased the demands for the colonel's removal. Hence, before the end of April 1945, about one month after the trial, Crandall was removed from his post, placed on terminal leave, and then retired.[45]

During the course of the trial and its review, both Mary McLeod Bethune and Eleanor Roosevelt individually sought an audience with Colonel Hobby. The latter ended up talking to Lieutenant Colonel Westray Boyce, who was later to succeed Hobby as director. Colonel Hobby was called to the White House to discuss the Lovell situation. And Congressman William T. Granaham, among others, asked Secretary of War Stimson for more information about the case; he wanted to know what could be done to prevent the assignment of "dirty work" to blacks.[46]

Charles H. Houston, a prominent civil rights lawyer, likewise was interested in seeing that black WACs not be given discriminatory job assignments. He suggested that the National Council of Negro Women investigate Lovell to make sure that the conditions the blacks had complained about were eradicated. Houston, however, was just as much interested in the record of the case, and believed that the defense could have more effectively developed and presented evidence of discrimination. He also thought that the defendants' company commander, who took the position that their grievances were not substantial, should have taken the time to convince the women of that or protested the discrimination. Carl Murphy, president of the *Afro-American,* decried the discriminatory job assignments of blacks, but he was most concerned about the retention of Colonel Crandall as commandant, especially after the women were restored to duty.[47]

This case embarrassed both the War Department and the corps; both had tried to avoid publicity which would reflect adversely on the corps. After the War Department's inspector general's office confirmed in a confidential report that blacks and non-blacks at Lovell were not given the same assignments, all of the black WACs at Fort Devens were transferred to Fort Des Moines.[48]

After the case was resolved, one of the black officers at Fort Des Moines, in a confidential letter dated April 4, 1945, thanked the NAACP for its "active interest and unrelenting fight in behalf of the four Negro WACs who were tried and severely sentenced at Ft. Devens, Mass." The writer felt that the assistance given to the women by the NAACP "will encourage, lift the morale, and inspire Brown WACs all over this country and abroad." At this time a unit of black WACs was in England. The officer then spelled out what she regarded as a most important missing link between black units in field assignments and WAC headquarters:

> We hope that the investigation which you made in connection with this case will reveal to the War Department that some liaison is needed between Negro units in the field and WAC Headquarters. Since Major Harriet West has been transferred completely from the WAC Section, all liaison between the two has ended. White WAC Service Command Directors have been ineffective in this matter; hence a Negro staff field worker is imperatively needed. With such a worker the Devens situation might have been adequately investigated and adjusted without the trouble that developed there.[49]

The officer stated that the black WACs were "doing a job of which you may well be proud" and that they only wanted an opportunity to serve "without intimidation and to the fullest extent of their capacity and training." After requesting that her communication be kept confidential, she expressed deep gratitude for the interest and effort the NAACP had given to blacks in the military.[50]

Three WACs who were set upon and beaten by local police in a Kentucky bus station were also court-martialed. This case was probably one of the most bizarre and ludicrous to go before a military court. The women involved were Pfc Helen Smith of Syracuse, New York, Pfc Georgia Boston of Dallas, Texas, and Private Tommie Smith of Lexington, Kentucky. Pfc Helen Smith, whose husband was a veteran of World War I and whose son was then a corporal in the army on overseas duty, entered a Greyhound station in Elizabethtown, Kentucky, to wait for a bus to take her to Fort Knox. The section of the waiting room designated Colored was crowded, so, Pfc Smith sat on a bench as close as possible to the Colored section. She was joined on the bench by a few other black WACs who also were returning to Fort Knox. All of the women were in uniform.[51]

A local policeman entered the bus station and ordered, "Git up and git out of here! This place ain't for niggers. This place is for white people." Pfc Smith started to explain that the other section was crowded, but the policeman insisted that the "niggers git up and git out." When they did not move immediately, the policeman declared that he would arrest them. At this point, Pfc Smith asked him to call the military police. The policeman angrily responded that he didn't need any military police to handle the "nigger wenches." Then one of the other black WACs told the policeman that she had heard enough of the "nigger business," which was too much from a "smart northerner" (who really was a Southerner by birth and upbringing) and induced the policeman to begin beating her over the head with his billy. Pfc Smith sent the third WAC for the military police and then went to the aid of the one under attack.[52]

The women were brutally beaten with billies and black-jacks by two civilian policemen. One of the women was dragged across the floor while being hit about the head. Pfc Smith, who was incarcerated in the local jail immediately following the incident, was beaten so badly that she was in the hospital for a week before she was able to relate what had happened. What was really incredible to the three WACs was that not a single individual in that crowded waiting room stepped forward to answer their calls for help or to call off the thugs.[53]

When the battered and beaten women arrived on the post, they were confronted with court-martial charges. They were reprimanded and charged with violating the state's jim crow laws and, of all things, assaulting police officers. Before the case was heard by a special court-martial in August 1945, Colonel R. C. Throckmorton, the post commander at Fort Knox, had to change one of the specifications to disorderly conduct after protesting local black leaders pointed out to him that the state had no jim crow laws for bus stations and public buildings. The women were officially charged with violating Article Ninety-six of the Articles of War—being disorderly in a public place while in uniform.[54]

The two civilian policemen, the perpetrators of the heinous racist beatings, were the chief witnesses for the prosecution. Some of the non-black residents of Elizabethtown also showed up to testify on the disorderly conduct specification. Fortunately for the women, the seven-member court judged the case on its merits and returned a verdict of not guilty.[55] The army had explained to inquiring black leaders that by prior agreement with the local authorities it took legal action against the women to keep the case out of the local courts. After the case had been resolved in the military court, the black leaders wanted the War Department to prosecute the two policemen for assaulting and attacking the women. The War Department disclaimed jurisdiction in the case and suggested that the black leaders themselves pursue the matter with the United States Department of Justice or the attorney general of the State of Kentucky. William Warley, editor of the *Louisville News,* regarded the failure of the War Department to take legal action against the policemen as a "white wash" and strongly criticized the army for refusing to protect the civil rights of its personnel or seek punishment for the wrongs inflicted on them.[56]

Two years earlier—on November 3, 1943—the civilian aide to the secretary of war in a lengthy memorandum urged the War Department to support legislation then before Congress which would have extended federal authority to deal with cases involving the type of treatment visited upon the three women at the Kentucky bus station. The memorandum was prepared with a view toward the 1944 presidential election, in which there had already been indications that the treatment of blacks in the military would be "the most important issue" in the Republican party "effort to capture the Negro vote." The civilian aide pointed out that political pressure in the final days of the 1940 campaign had led to the appointment of a black civilian aide to the secretary of war and a statement that blacks would be included in the army air force, and that there had been no prior planning for the latter. Although he acknowledged that the military should keep out of politics, the aide suggested it would be wise "to recognize and anticipate the political situation and take immediate steps to prevent the necessity for drastic action next summer."[57] The aide was referring to the rush job the army had to do to plan for and put into operation the black air force unit.

The civilian aide noted, among other things, that the House of Representatives had passed a bill which provided punishment for anyone who assaulted or killed federal officers (military personnel by definition were federal officers), and he suggested that the War Department should urge the Senate to approve the measure. He frankly stated, "While the passage of this legislation will not eliminate attacks on Negro military personnel, the legislation itself will do much to express the official attitude of the Federal Government and the War Department toward these regrettable incidents."[58] More importantly, the aide advised:

> After the passage of this legislation Negro troops, whenever possible, should be moved from the South. General [Benjamin O.] Davis [Sr.] and I are in agreement that this would be a most desirable step. We both feel that all publicity to this effect be strenuously avoided. However, our recent trips into the South indicate clearly that little, if anything, can be expected when men are constantly subjected to the types of practices they run into in many southern communities. It should be emphasized that southern as well as northern Negroes dislike these practices.[59]

The civilian aide's recommendations went further than those of any other Pentagon official, but Secretary Stimson did not have a high opinion of blacks, and it was too much to expect him to do them any favors. Besides, these motions had come from a black. Heretofore, as in the Kentucky bus station incident, the military customarily turned its back on the civilian perpetrators of racist attacks. Harriet West and George F. Martin, the director of the WAAC control division, some six months prior to the civilian aide's memorandum had proposed that Northern WAACs not be assigned to Southern installations. As late as February 1945, the Third Service Command WAC Civilian Advisory Committee repeated a suggestion it had made two years earlier and urged that "negro women from the South be assigned to stations in the South since they are accustomed to the social patterns" and that "negro women from the North should be sent only to WAC units outside the South."[60] The civilian aide's recommendation went beyond those of West, Martin, and the Civilian Advisory Committee, and placed on the record that blacks—both Southern and Northern—resented the "southern way of life" and that their morale and efficiency were negatively affected by Southern "practices." But the status quo prevailed.

Jim crow laws, discriminatory job assignments, racial incidents, and isolation on Southern posts led some black WACs to seek relief or resign from the service. For example, "a very unhappy, disillusioned WAC officer" told the civilian aide to the secretary of war that morale among blacks stationed in the South had reached "rock bottom." She explained that WACs and soldiers were subjected to Southern race prejudice and hate. She had hoped to have been rotated out of the South in accord with a "promise" made to her. An enlisted woman found the situation at Camp Forrest in Tennessee and its surrounding area so discriminatory and racially unpleasant that she wanted to know why we were fighting the war.[61]

Then there was Private Ana Aikens, who enrolled in the corps in February 1943. After basic training at Fort Des Moines, she had field assignments at Fort Clark (Texas), Camp Gruber (Oklahoma), and Fort Sam Houston (Texas). She confronted segregated seats in the theaters, Whites Only signs at the bowling alleys and skating rinks, off-limit nightclubs, civilian bus drivers who were the law, insensitive and even hostile post personnel, and discriminatory job assignments. Private Aikens regarded Fort Des Moines as the best of her locations. There, she said, blacks had to deal only with segregated service clubs. She stated that "camping colored soldiers and WACs in Southern States offers complications, inconveniences and much personal feeling which hinder progress." She talked about the racial hatred and vengeful attitude of Southern whites and concluded with the remark that "until we are able to live together as a people, colored units should be sheltered from the inconveniences of the South." After more than two years in the service, practically all of it in the South, Private Aikens got fed up, resigned from the corps, and returned to Washington, D.C., to resume her education.[62]

The black WACs disapproved of discrimination, the flip side of the army's segregation policy. The army had pledged that discrimination would not occur, and when it did, the women sought relief, wrote letters, sent telegrams, resigned from the volunteer service, and even staged strikes. Opposed to segregation in the corps from the very beginning, black leaders, organizations, and press complained about, criticized, and protested. Bethune especially gave substantial support and assistance to the black women in the corps when they confronted racial incidents. She and other black leaders were the guardian angels of the black WACs.

4. BLACK UNITS AND FIELD ASSIGNMENTS

In assigning women to the field, requests that would relieve enlisted men or army officers for combat duty were given preference. After that, requests from the Aircraft Warning Service were filled. The women also could be used to replace army civil servants when vacancies existed and then only when "it proved impracticable to secure civilian" replacements, in which event, War Department approval would be needed before the women could be assigned as civilian replacements.[1] In each instance, the request for the women's employment came from the field—from the bottom up and not from the top down. This was standard army operating procedure posited on the premise that the field commanders knew their needs better than those not on location.

Hence the location, reception, and employment of the women in the corps—both black and non-black—in a very large measure, depended on the willingness of commanding officers in the field to request them and on the attitude of these field commanders and their staff toward women in the service. In view of the social climate at that time, this state of affairs affected black women more acutely than non-blacks. The corps ran into this problem with the Aircraft Warning Service, and as early as February 1943, the director of the corps acknowledged to the civilian aide to the secretary of war that they had to give "further study" to the possible use of trained black WAAC personnel.[2]

On April 1, 1943, the army's adjutant general circulated a confidential letter on the "expansion and utilization" of WAACs, in which he stated that black WAAC personnel would be allocated to the service commands on the basis of the number of blacks recruited from each service command and the needs of the several service commands. Each service command was ordered to "report by 20 April 1943, the maximum total number of negro WAAC personnel which can be absorbed by your command."[3]

At that time, a significant number of unassigned black WAACs were at the training centers, especially at Fort Des Moines. On April 19, 1943, 742 blacks who had finished basic training were without assignments and were regarded as unassignable unless they had additional training. About a month later, 842 were available for assignment with 530 of them available since May 1, 1943. On June 30, 1943, 623 blacks at Fort Des Moines were without assignments. Of these, 127 had graduated from administration school, 150 others had graduated from cooks and bakers school, and another 21 had completed motor transport school. Some of the rest who had completed basic training and had no additional schooling had military occupational specialities. At the same time, another 260 blacks who had completed basic training at Fort Devens were unassigned. On July 14, 1943, 832 women at Fort Des Moines were unassigned or awaiting assignments. Of these, 212 were waiting for the organization of their cadre and transportation to the field. Another 239 at Fort Devens were unassigned. As of July 14, 1943, 861 women were completely without assignments.[4]

The service commands were not very responsive to the order to "report by 20 April 1943, the maximum total number of negro WAAC personnel which could be absorbed" in their commands. And plans to establish a "colored" motor transport school at Fort Devens to train 700 of the unassigned women were scrapped. Questions were raised about a market for the women once they were trained, about the availability of black male or female instructors, about whether the course would parallel the one at Fort Des Moines, about whether the course would be longer and more thorough than the existing one, and about the overall inflow of the students. Harriet M. West favored the establishment of the school as a means of getting the women trained and assigned.[5]

West made a tour of the Sixth and Seventh Service Commands to see if she could interest the field commanders in taking some of the unassigned black women. She stopped first at Fort Des Moines and noted the crowded conditions in the staging area where the women were sent after basic training to await assignments. She stated that Colonel McCoskrie also was desirous of sending the women out because of the crowded conditions. She next talked with the commanding officer of the Seventh Service Command, who asked about stationing a black laundry company at Fort Riley (Kansas). West advised him that no laundry companies, either black nor non-black, were approved for the WAACs. At Fort Riley, the post commander repeated the request for a laundry company, but said that he understood that laundry companies were not approved. He then stated that he could use possibly 230 women as a hospital unit. The post commander at Fort Leonard Wood (Missouri) said he "could use 300 immediately if they could be used in the laundry." West inquired how he would use them in the laundry, and indicated that such jobs as checking, sorting, and bundling clean clothes might be satisfactory. She also suggested the use of the women in the hospital, in the salvage shop, and as clerks and messengers. Before West left, the post commander at Fort Leonard Wood agreed to requisition 150 women for use in the hospital and in black units as clerks and messengers.[6]

West found the commanders at Fort Sheridan (Illinois) and at Fort Custer (Michigan) more receptive. At Fort Sheridan, the commanding officer said he was willing to use black WAACs wherever they were qualified to serve. He indicated that he intended to requisition 66 women. The commanding officer at Fort Custer had assignments available for 117 non-specialists, or basics, whom he would use at the checking station and as typists in the insurance office.[7]

Possibly reflecting the number of blacks who reportedly made low scores on the AGCT, the backlog of unassigned blacks, and her recent trip to the field installations, about ten days later, West made a series of recommendations to the director of the control division. She suggested that enrollment be denied to those who scored below the average on the military aptitude test and who did not have at least two years of high school. She advised that "a thorough analysis" of "the customs or social conditions in the different sections of the country" was "imperative" before requests for assignments of blacks were honored. She asked that the attitude of the field commanders toward having black women in their commands be taken into account. She also believed that facts should be ascertained about the "suitability and adequacy of housing arrangements, working conditions, and types of assignments," as well as the social environment the women would have to deal with in their off-duty hours. West noted that "as far as practicable" the women should be assigned "to areas from which they came." Finally, she urged that these analyses be made "to prevent any unpleasantness that would give unfavorable publicity to the Corps."[8]

In the meantime, Major George F. Martin, the director of the control division, toured the same installations that West had visited: Fort Des Moines, Fort Riley, Fort Leonard Wood, Fort Sheridan, and Fort Custer. At Fort Des Moines, he noted from the availability reports the number of black women who had scored in grades IV and V on the AGCT and concluded that it was going to be "difficult" to sell a large number of them to field commanders. Hence, he thought that the corps should make a "decision" to use them in laundries, hospital messes, salvage and reclamation stations, as checkers at induction stations, and in the processing of clothing. He stated that many of these black women "are of such inferior quality, not only in ability, but in character that the standard of the Corps, as a whole, will be lowered when these enrollees are sent into the field." He suggested the "hand-picking" of personnel and posts: "If southern camps are used, southern enrollees be assigned to these posts," since they could better understand and cope with the situation there.[9]

Martin said that his visit to the field installations revealed that some commanders "are at a loss to determine how" black personnel can be used other than in "laundries, mess units, or salvage and reclamation shops." He felt that in assigning black women to these types of jobs, the corps and the army would expose themselves to criticism. He therefore recommended screening at the training centers all unassigned AGCT grade IV and V women for the purpose of discharging them from the service for the convenience of the government. He further recommended that no applicants in grade V be accepted in the corps and that the recruiting of blacks be "informally" curtailed.[10]

Major Martin's recommendation on informally curtailing the recruitment of blacks, and another on holding a conference with black recruiting officers to discuss the problem, were crossed out, perhaps by someone at a higher level.[11] Martin apparently came to these conclusions, even the one on the quality of the character of the women, from observing availability reports at Fort Des Moines and talking with non-black commanding officers and their staffs about how they would employ black women.

Some requisitions for blacks could not be filled. Camp Carson in Colorado requested seventy-five black women, with the requirement that sixty-six of them had to be motor transport school graduates. Since the corps at that time only had twenty-one motor transport school graduates available, the request had to be placed on hold until more blacks had completed the program. Camp Shelby in Mississippi and Camp Rucker in Alabama wanted units composed entirely of Southern blacks. Officials at the training center were "told to free" the requisitions from Camp Shelby and Camp Rucker.[12] Blacks were subsequently stationed there, and available records do not reveal whether they were Southern blacks.

The corps had no problem placing the first two black companies that completed basic training. They were sent to Fort Huachuca (Arizona), where the all-black Ninety-second Division was stationed, arrived on December 2, 1942, and were given a red-carpet reception. They marched to their quarters to the accompaniment of a band and amid well-wishers who lined up along the route.[13]

The 300 women who made up the two companies at Fort Huachuca had their own mess, a large recreational hall, and barracks area. The companies had their mess officer, Annie L. Brown, one of the first two blacks to have graduated from Mess Officers School. In their off-duty hours, the women had access to the theater, service clubs, social activities, and recreational centers on the post, including the basketball court.[14]

At Fort Huachuca, the women worked as typists, stenographers, and clerks. They drove vehicles and served as chauffeurs, messengers, telephone operators, and librarians. They operated the theaters and the service clubs. They were

Standing retreat at Fort Huachuca.

medical, laboratory, and surgical technicians, physical therapists, and ward attendants. Some were even employed in light
motor vehicle maintenance. There were no jobs or positions
off-limits to them except those prescribed for all WACs.[15]

The post commander at Fort Huachuca commended the
women several times for their competence, diligence, cooper-
ation and moral character. In May 1943, on the first anni-
versary of the establishment of the corps, Colonel Edwin N.
Hardy, the post commander, said of them, "These young
women are showing marked ability and genius in taking over
essential jobs from able-bodied men.". He spoke of the "keen
competition" they gave the men in the observance of military
customs, courtesy, and discipline. He said that "all of us are
glad to have the Waacs at Fort Huachuca." He concluded with
the statement that the women "are proving of real value in
our war effort at their stations." The officers on the post
believed that the women made a tremendous contribution to
the operation of the command and to the war effort.[16]

At Fort Sam Houston, one of the posts where Private
Aikens was stationed, the black unit was originally brought in
to open up a center for servicemen returning from overseas
duty. The army, however, changed its plans, and the women
were assigned jobs in the shipping depot as truck jumpers,
messengers, typists, and shipping clerks—jobs that were
created for them and that placed them in an unpleasant
relationship with civilian employees at the depot. Non-black
WACs at Fort Sam Houston—there were two companies of
them there—worked at a variety of jobs at the headquarters,
photographic laboratory, signal corps, post hospital, and
elsewhere. Blacks were not permitted to work in any capacity
at Brooke General Hospital; instead, the black WACs were
confined to the shipping depot where they were made to feel
uncomfortable, resented by the civilian employees.[17]

The post commander at Fort Riley (as he had told Harriet
M. West during her tour of inquiry) had requisitioned two
hundred women. The company was activated on August 26,
1943, and was one of the largest black WAC companies in the
United States during World War II. The women worked at
the hospital on the post as ward orderlies, ward attendants,
nurses' aides, physiotherapy aides, and medical, surgical,

dental, and laboratory technicians. They also worked in the hospital mess as mess attendants and mess sergeants.[18]

On a staff visit to Fort Riley in October 1943, Harriet M. West found that the assignments of the women were satisfactory and their morale on the whole was good. West praised the commanding officer who, she judged, was doing an excellent job in seeking reassignments for those women who were misassigned. West also praised the commanding officer for administering to the material needs of her troops. In West's opinion, the commanding officer was eager to be a good company officer, but she thought that the commander was too lenient in some instances in dealing with the concerns of the women and not sympathetic enough in other instances. West believed that this inconsistency was due to a lack of self-confidence occasioned in part by the presence of a very talented and aggressive junior officer. This inconsistency apparently resulted in the court-martial of some enlisted women in the company for failure to obey the company commander's orders.[19]

The post commander at Fort Sheridan (Illinois) had indicated his willingness to use blacks in positions for which they were qualified. He had said that he would request sixty-six. In all, eighty-three were stationed there and employed in a variety of jobs. Almost all of them did clerical work or were technicians. They operated graphotype machines, processed soldiers' records, and worked in personnel. One was a bugler. Seventy-nine were high school graduates, and more than thirty had some college education. Additionally, twenty-five (or almost one-third) of them scored in group II on the AGCT.[20]

In September 1944, the inspector general's office made on-the-spot probes of the morale and unit efficiency of black WAC companies at Fort Benning (Georgia), Camp Forrest (Tennessee), Camp Breckenridge and Fort Knox (Kentucky) and Camp Claiborne (Louisiana). At Fort Benning, the morale of the women was rated very good. They had no complaints, and the post commander reported that they "were well disciplined, interested in executing their duties properly, and that their conduct and behavior were excellent." The women worked as typists and file clerks at the reception center and postal section, and many worked at the station hospital.[21]

At Camp Forrest, the black company commander stated that the company's morale was good and so were the recreational facilities. She mentioned that the soldiers who had been a problem had been shipped out and that only the station complement was then on the post. The post commander stated that "ninety-five percent" of the black WACs "are doing an excellent job and are supplying technicians in every department of the hospital." But he wanted to take care of the other five percent through court-martial "if present restrictions on punishment by court-martial are lifted." The medical officer at the hospital, where all of the blacks worked except the company cadre, stated that 33 of the 168 were not doing a satisfactory job. He said that at that time they were seeking discharges for two of those doing unsatisfactory work "under Section VIII"—mental instability, incompetence, or incapacity.[22]

Both the medical officer at Camp Forrest and the inspector general's team felt that there should have been an opportunity for women with superior ability to advance. They cited the case of Sergeant Theresa N. McDuffie, a black, who had all of the qualifications for a commissioned dietitian except prior training in a civilian hospital. Both recommended that she be given credit for the experience that she had already gained at an army hospital and be commissioned.[23]

The commanding officer at Camp Breckenridge said that the WACs had been doing an excellent job, but (apparently influenced by some members of the black male unit on the post) "there has been a lessening of the proper attitude by a minority group." The post surgeon, under whom most of the women worked, also attested to their excellent performance, but he likewise noted a decline in efficiency. He said, "Their work is still fair, but they have lost interest." Six of the WACs assigned to post headquarters, according to their supervisor, continued to do an excellent job. Captain Myrtle E. Anderson, the CO of the WAC unit, attributed the poor morale to personality clashes within the unit and believed that the situation was only temporary.[24]

The state of affairs at Camp Breckenridge was an improvement over previous conditions. An earlier report pointed out a number of "irregularities" in the assignments of the black enlisted women (there were two non-black units on the post). The inspector found thirty blacks working in the laundry, which was operated entirely by civilians. Although most of the thirty had been former laundry workers, they were dissatisfied with their assignments. Moreover, the corps discouraged the assignment of its members to laundry work and as replacements for civilian workers except in unusual cases. The inspector also found fifteen blacks working as hostesses, cashiers, soda jerks, and dishwashers in the service club, and he stated that two women in the service club were enough. Most surprising to the inspector was that five "well educated negro enrolled women" who were "administration school graduates" were "employed sweeping warehouses." The inspector, who had been the first commandant at the WAC Training Center at Fort Des Moines, concluded his report by noting that a non-black WAC officer, who had arrived at Camp Breckenridge just a few days earlier and had the confidence of the post headquarters there, was correcting the improper assignments at the post hospital.[25]

The post commander and the surgeon at Fort Knox both reported that the morale of the women was very good and that they "were doing well and earning their way." Earlier the situation at Fort Knox had not been good. The women had been requisitioned for kitchen help; they were sent out as non-specialists, or basics (as most blacks were), and they were virtually permanent KPs. The executive officer at the hospital on the post refused to use them on the hospital wards, and it was the view of the corps's visiting officer that the women "will have to do what" they were "sent to do" since there was "no other unit on the post where colored WAACs could be used."[26]

This officer attributed the problem to the "glamourized ideas" of most of the women about the jobs they should have had. She stated that as kitchen help "most of these girls are much better off now than they were in civilian life." She identified three of the women as agitators and thought that the post commander should discharge them and any others who refused to work. She asserted that "this colored company needs strong leadership, a company commander who will strictly enforce military discipline."[27] The post commander, however, was more understanding of the women's concerns. He did not want misassignments and indicated a willingness "to make any necessary adjustments in assignments."[28]

The morale of the women at Camp Claiborne was poor. They cited transportation among their worst problems and stated that they "take a taxi costing five dollars" in order "to prevent being humiliated." The inspector reported that some of the women would "try to get out [of the service] with a disability discharge, while they would stay if conditions were better." The post commander at Camp Claiborne said that the blacks appeared "to be dissatisfied with their assignments and treatment," that "most of them had a bad attitude," and that "they are race conscious and feel that they were being discriminated against." Their job ratings, in the view of the post commander, ranged from excellent to unsatisfactory.[29]

At Fort Clark (Texas), the women had relatively good assignments and their morale was relatively good. The conditions on the post were tolerable, but they had to deal with a racist off-post environment. With the arrival of a new post commandant, the situation deteriorated. The new man installed separate doors at the rear of the theater, post exchange, and bowling alleys for blacks to use. Separate seating arrangements were ordained in the chapel, separate trucks and buses were used to carry the women to work, and the ratings were frozen.[30]

To show their displeasure with the imposition of additional jim crow devices, blacks stopped attending chapel for two weeks. Then, on Easter Day, 1944, when a new chaplain preached his first sermon, a number of black WACs (including two officers and the black WAC choir) attended and sat in the forbidden sections of the chapel. The black choir, which normally occupied the loft in the rear, sat in the front pews on the whites-only side of the chapel. The following Sunday, the blacks resumed their boycott of the church services. The post commander believed that the whole episode was a conspiracy and suspected that the two WAC chaplain's assistants were the leaders.[31]

The members of the black unit at Fort McClellan (Alabama) in mid-1943 suffered from misassignments and a lack of clearly defined jobs and chains of command. Thirty-nine of them worked in the service club, including four in the service club library, fourteen in the post office, four in officers mess, four as maids in a civilian dormitory, two as drivers for the unit, and eighteen were carried as overhead. The maids were pulled off the job and assigned as substitutes in the service club after remarks by the visiting officer.[32]

The sergeant in charge of the service club workers, who was a member of the unit, had to report each morning to the service club personnel to find out the daily assignments for the women. The sergeant than relayed the information to the squad or section leaders of each detail. Moreover, the civilian hostess of the service club and the assistant special service club officer (a male) "always" gave the women additional chores in the course of their daily tour of duty. The result was that the women did not know whom to take orders from or what they were going to do from hour to hour and from day to day.[33]

The post commander told the reporting officer that the women "should take orders from the sergeant" in charge of the service workers "through their squad leaders," and the confusion continued. The post commander had previously stated that the women did not have to wax any more floors with the heavy machines, but apparently, the assistant special service officer did not get the message. He would have had some of the women charged with a court-martial offense had not the unit's commanding officer rushed to the scene to straighten out the matter—army policy is to obey the order and ask questions later. Further, the post commander revealed to the reporting staff officer that he thought that white officers should have been assigned as cadre of the black detachment and was dissatisfied when he discovered that the officer cadre was black. But he confessed that he was "very satisfied with" the black company commander's "ability to do her job since she took command." The visiting staff officer judged that the situation at Fort McClellan was in need of improvement and that the company's commanding officer was the right person for that job.[34]

The second group of WAACs to arrive at Walla Walla, August 2, 1943.

The Walla Walla Base was the first army air force facility to receive blacks. Interviewed by the local press one week after their arrival, the women expressed satisfaction with their assignment. Speaking for the group, one woman told the reporter: "We think this is a wonderful field. We like our barracks, day room, mess hall and we like our work here." Reportedly, the women in the group assigned to this air base in the state of Washington were all graduates of the WAAC Administration School at Fort Des Moines except for the mess personnel. Some, if not all, of the latter had presumably completed the course at the Cooks and Bakers School at Fort Des Moines, as that was the army requirement.[35]

Seven weeks after their tour of duty had begun at Walla Walla, the base commander, Lieutenant Colonel Harry E. Gilmore, remarked, "The spirit of the WACs on this base is best evidenced by the fact that all but four of the original company re-enlisted for the duration." He added, "These girls are intelligent and capable workers, and a credit to the uniform which they wear [and] they are fast becoming an invaluable aid to the officers and departments throughout the base command."[36]

When Gilmore spoke, more than seventy-five of the women had been assigned to permanent jobs on the base, mostly to clerical positions at base headquarters, or technical jobs at the base hospital, photographic laboratory, or ordnance department. At base headquarters, they worked in the personnel section, the message center, the mimeograph section, the photographic section, the supply section, the chemical room, and the mail room. At the base hospital, they served as medical and surgical assistants or technicians, nurses' aides, and dental assistants. Others had permanent assignments as sheet metal workers and parachute inspectors. Forty other women were taking a special advanced course in typing and shorthand at St. Vincent's Academy in the city of Walla Walla and were expected to be assigned to post headquarters.[37]

At Douglas Army Air Field, the second army air force facility to have a black WAC unit, the women packed parachutes, assisted in the maintenance of aircraft, did general office work, and worked in the photographic section. Others were assigned to the base hospital. The commanding officer said of them, "I've found them cooperative at all times and their enthusiasm, industry, attention to duty and conduct make them a real asset to this post." He added that "in several cases" the women's "efficiency and spirit were highly praised by base commanders."[38]

The unit at Wendover Air Field in Utah began its duty in December 1943. Its personnel consisted of women who had had their basic training at Fort Des Moines and Fort Devens and included the WACs who had been stationed at Walla Walla. On the base, the women served in many types of military occupational specialities and in many of the sections and offices, including the hospital. They worked in the classification office, base headquarters, quartermaster supply, personnel office, photographic laboratory, chemical office, and physical training department. In these sections, they did clerical work or were technicians. At the base hospital, they

Top: Participating in a War Loan Drive. *Bottom:* First Sergeant Minnie B. Gay on the job at Walla Walla.

served as medical, surgical, and laboratory technicians. One of the WACs played the organ at the base chapel and was the chaplain's assistant.[39]

Most, if not all, of the women at Wendover Field were transferred to the air base at Sioux City, Iowa, on April 1, 1944. They were met on their arrival by the post band and given an enthusiastic welcome. The second largest WAC unit in the Second Army Air Force, the black detachment replaced a company of women who had been shipped out. According to an article in the *Sioux City Sunday Journal,* the women in the unit were mainly from the Atlantic seaboard states, their average age was twenty-four, and their average intelligence test score was above 108. Reportedly, one-fourth of the women had intelligence test scores of over 110. The newspaper article further revealed that a significant number of the women had been schoolteachers and government workers.[40]

At the Sioux City Air Base, a majority of the women were clerical workers at the personnel, postal and public relations offices. Others served at the message center, in the ordnance section, in quartermaster supply, in the photographic laboratory, in parachute repair, and in the air inspection section. At the base hospital, they were ward workers, and medical, surgical, and dental technicians. One was a certified engine mechanic and others had received on-the-job training as lathe operators and parachute riggers.[41]

In their spare time, many either participated in or enjoyed watching athletic events. The unit's choral group, which previously had performed at Wendover Field and had performed on a local radio station in Salt Lake City, hoped to continue its activities in Sioux City. They also had plans to hold dances and informal social gatherings for their civilian friends in the city as well as for the airmen on the base.[42]

By the end of 1944, black detachments were located at three other army air force facilities: Midland in Texas, Fresno in California, and Laurinburg-Maxton in North Carolina. Other black units were stationed at other air force installations later (see Appendix 5 for black units, their assignments, and their commanding officers). Altogether, blacks in these units performed jobs in at least thirty-five different military occupational specialities. Most of them had arrived at the air

Two women take their turn at bat in a softball game at Walla Walla.

force stations as basics or straight out of basic training and had acquired skills and job classifications by on-the-job training.[43]

A staff report on the black WAC unit at Fort Dix (New Jersey) apparently caused some concern at headquarters in Washington. The report, dated July 19, 1943, stated that a majority of the blacks in the company were expected to opt out of the service when the corps converted to an integral part of the Army of the United States. The report noted that "quite a number of them are working in the Station Hospital as permanent Mess Attendants, which appears to be another name for KP." The report also mentioned that ratings or promotions seemed to have been frozen, yet in the view of the staff officer the morale of the women was rated fair.[44]

This less than favorable report probably led to some changes in job assignments for blacks at Fort Dix. An enlisted woman who joined the corps in July 1943 took her basic training at Fort Devens, and went to Motor Transport School in Des Moines, and was stationed at Fort Dix for eighteen months. Her first job was a detail to the hospital as a driver, occasionally for Colonel Harvey Fitzgerald, the hospital commandant. Some six weeks later, she was given a regular assignment to the "bakers' group" in the hospital mess. She was the bread truck driver and delivered bread, pastry, cookies, and other bakery items to the mess halls, officers and service clubs, and other food dispensing outlets on the huge post. Other women in her unit worked as orderlies, ward attendants, nurse's aides, and technicians at Tilden General Hospital and as typists and clerks elsewhere on the post.[45]

This enlisted woman spent her last months in the service at the army air force installations in Midland and Amarillo, Texas. She said, "I stayed on both bases the whole time and spent my off-duty hours at the segregated service club, the segregated non-commissioned officers club, and in the barracks." The black WACs at Midland and Amarillo were assigned to a variety of jobs.[46]

The first black unit assigned to the Fifth Service Command arrived at Camp Atterbury (Indiana) on May 22, 1943. It was welcomed by the post commander, the company commander of the non-black WAAC headquarters company, other officers, and enlisted personnel. The 144 enlisted women and their 2 officers found their barracks ready to receive them, compliments of one of the non-black WAAC officers and a detail of enlisted women. A status report over a year later stated that the women in the black unit were working throughout the hospital, their work was satisfactory, they were well-adjusted, they messed at the hospital, and their barracks were "entirely adequate." The report further noted that the women had an attractive recreation room and a well-planned recreational program.[47]

In March 1944 this unit was redesignated as the Twenty-first WAC Hospital Company and continued to work at Wakeman General Hospital on the post at Camp Atterbury. The women were assigned to jobs as ward attendants, medical and surgical technicians, and clerks. Most of them were directly involved in the care of the sick and wounded.[48]

Some of the women at Camp Atterbury had second jobs, as members of the glee club, which made frequent public appearances. So well did the glee club perform and so well was it received that it was used to assist in recruiting not only in Indiana but also in Ohio. The women at Wakeman General Hospital, then, were contributing on two fronts to the war effort: caring for the sick and wounded and recruiting—and doing both with competence and enthusiasm. In recognition of its work, the unit was awarded the Commander's Plaque for outstanding service.[49]

The black company at Camp Maxey (Texas) won a Meritorious Unit Award for its sustained effort and endurance in rendering service to the victims of a typhoon, which virtually destroyed the nearby town of Antlers, Oklahoma, in 1945. The women stayed at their stations in the hospital twenty-four hours without a break administering to the victims, then, with only a few hours rest, returned to duty, assisting the victims and carrying on with their regular assignments at the hospital.[50]

For the detachment at Gardiner General Hospital in Chicago, Illinois, the War Department's plan called for the training of eighty-five medical and surgical technicians at Fort Oglethorpe (Georgia) and for the selection of additional women from within the corps to bring the total strength of the company up to a hundred enlisted women. To house the

black unit at Gardiner, which was located on fashionable Lake
Shore Drive with a view of Lake Michigan, the federal
government had leased park property adjacent to the hospital
from the city of Chicago. But by the early part of April 1945,
when the accommodations for the black unit were about 90
percent completed, the War Department realized that it had
a serious problem on its hands.[51]

Protests from wealthy individuals, from the surrounding
community, from real estate groups, and from business
associations had become more vociferous and persistent.
These individuals and groups strongly objected to the quar-
tering of blacks in the exclusive "restricted white residential
area." They complained about the "unsightly" temporary
barracks being an eyesore along Lake Shore Drive. Most of
all, they did not want blacks near or in the whites-only beach,
asserting that the black women would attract black men to the
location and the presence of both might lead to racial
violence. And they complained that blacks in the area would
lower property values.[52]

The protesters took their concerns to the mayor of Chicago, the commanding general of the Sixth Service Command, the deputy chief of staff for the service commands at
the Pentagon, and the assistant secretary of war. They wanted
the army to send the black WACs elsewhere or, at least, to
relocate their barracks. In their complaints, the protesters
conjured up images of the bloody 1919 race riot in Chicago,
the worst of the racial violence which swept the nation in what
has been dubbed the "Red Summer." The riot in Chicago was
sparked by the killing of a black youth by a hail of stones when
he crossed the imaginary line separating the black from white
bathing areas of Lake Michigan.[53]

The activity of the protesters to keep the WACs out of the
area inspired the black community leaders in Chicago and
groups advocating racial justice to urge the army to proceed
with its plan to bring in the WACs. The Chicago and
Northern District Federation of Colored Women's Clubs, the
Board of Directors of the National Council of Negro
Women, the Chicago Council Against Racial and Religious
Discrimination, and other groups and individuals held meet-

ings, sent letters, adopted resolutions, and met with officials to counter the action of the protesters.[54]

The army decided to activate the company, reasoning that relocation of the barracks would entail extra cost, place the women at a greater distance from their workplace, and still not remove the "hazard of racial incidents." Moreover, the army felt that it "must keep [its] pledge of original assignment" to the enlisted women—these women had been recruited specifically for assignment at Gardiner General Hospital, and the army had promised them that they would be assigned there. The War Department stood "ready to move" the women if trouble started, however. While the War Department was making its decision, the enlisted women who were to work at the hospital were housed with other WAC units at the Chicago Women's Civic Club Building.[55]

Designated as the Fifty-fifth WAC Hospital Company, the unit began its tour of duty at Gardiner in June 1945. The commandant of Gardiner General Hospital had reportedly said early on that he "had no use for WACs except as ward orderlies who he might use on cleaning and scrubbing duties." Perhaps there had been a change of command at Gardiner. Perhaps the critical shortage of experienced civilian health care personnel, the circumstance that the enlisted women had undergone a specialized training program, and the Lovell General Hospital case had changed some hospital commandants' attitudes toward the use of WACs, including black WACs. Perhaps because of the nature of the brouhaha surrounding the assignment of these particular WACs and of the knowledge that the Pentagon and others would be watching, the then-commandant of Gardiner General Hospital, Colonel John R. Hall, accepted the women as trained medical and surgical technicians and used them as such. And watching they were. Within a few months, the commanding general of the Sixth Service Command, Major General McCoach, along with the WAC service command director, Major Doris E. Epperson, visited the black unit. The mayor of Chicago, Edward J. Kelly, sent a message of "warm congratulations to [the unit] on your splendid achievement" and offered his "good wishes as you commence your noble work in the service of your country and humanity." The director of

A welcome reception for members of the 55th WAC Hospital Company, sponsored by a coalition of black organizations.

the WAC, Colonel Westray Battle Boyce, also paid a visit to the unit. In her letter to the unit's company commander, she wrote: "I want to tell you how very much I enjoyed my recent visit with you. It was indeed a pleasure to drop in on your detachment and to meet you."[56] With the attention these individuals and others paid to the unit, Colonel Hall probably considered that he should do his part to ensure its success.

Sylvia L. Cookman, who had been transferred from Fort Riley (Kansas) to take the position of first sergeant of the company, stated that being at Gardiner was a unique experience for that time: an all-black unit in a segregated military working in an all-white environment in which there was no overt or covert racial antagonism. Rosine Vance, who was a T/4 (a technical rank equivalent to sergeant) in the hospital complement of the company, concurred with Cookman's assessment. Vance also stated that the company's mess sergeant, Harriette O. Douglas, and her assistants prepared the "best spread" that she had eaten in the army, better than one could purchase at many expensive restaurants. T/4 Liniev Cryer, another member of the hospital complement, talked about the ratings or promotions that she and other women in the company received while at Gardiner General Hospital.[57]

Referring to the Fifty-fifth WAC Hospital Company, the official historian of the corps wrote:

> When it was planned to send a unit [of black WACs] to Gardiner General Hospital in Chicago, where a strained situation already existed, protests were received by the Army from four suburban civic groups, to the effect that stationing the women in a restricted white residential area, near a white bathing beach, might cause "incidents" and race riots. Although the Army ignored these protests and successfully stationed the unit at Gardiner General Hospital, such a community reaction obviously presented an adjustment problem to unit members.[58]

The only "protests" were those of the non-black citizens and civic groups. The army did not exactly ignore the protests of these groups. Nothing was mentioned in the statement

First Sergeant Sylvia L. Cookman, 55th WAC Hospital Company.

about the counterprotests of the black civic groups and individuals and the interracial council. The only success noted was that of stationing the unit in Chicago despite the protests. Nothing was said about the quality of the service rendered by the unit.

However, the Chicago Council Against Racial and Religious Discrimination, in a public statement, cited the unit "for the excellence of its work." The citation was made by prominent residents of the exclusive Lake Shore Drive area after the unit had departed. The residents apologized for the uninformed property and business groups who had protested and wanted the women to know that they would be welcomed back.

As noted above, Camp Rucker in Alabama had requested a company composed entirely of southern blacks and the post commander at Fort Des Moines was "told to free" that requisition. Several months later, in August 1943, a black company was sent to Camp Rucker. It cannot be ascertained whether all of the members of this company were southerners because the personnel records are not available. However, all three of the company's commissioned officers were from the South and so was the first sergeant.[59]

Thanksgiving Day Dinner, 1945, 55th WAC Hospital Company.

This company had trouble en route from Des Moines to Camp Rucker and had problems at Camp Rucker. Although provided with travel vouchers for Pullman accommodations and meal vouchers, the women were ordered by train officials to move to the jim crow coach when the train reached St. Louis, Missouri. The company commander, aware that there was no food service in the jim crow coach and that it was a long trip to Camp Rucker, could not talk the train officials into changing their minds and had the women leave the train. She then telephoned the commandant's office at Fort Des Moines and explained the situation. Arrangements were made to put up the women in St. Louis. Two days later, the group entrained to complete the trip to Camp Rucker by Pullman. However, the company commander and her supply and mess officer had no sleeping accommodations and had to sit the rest of the way.[60]

At Camp Rucker, the unit had its own quarters, mess hall, recreation area, and exercise area; it was a detachment as were most WAC units. The job assignments seem to have been made on the basis of the same rationale on which the request for an all-black southern complement was made. Many of the women had very menial jobs; some were not on the approved list for WACs. The company commander had some success in obtaining adjustments, some of them very respectable assignments, by personally talking to individuals in charge of the work stations. But, she got no satisfaction from lower echelon personnel for those women assigned to the nurses' quarters doing cleaning, making beds, performing general housekeeping chores, and rendering maid service. Army officers at post headquarters listened, but put her off. When she remarked that the problem was still not solved, she was ushered into the post commander's office. Before she could explain the problem and the circumstance that these assignment were not on the War Department's authorized list of jobs for WACs, the post commander, probably angered by some of the job changes that had been made, declared: "You have no detachment!"[61]

The company was deactivated. Its tour of duty at Camp Rucker lasted a little over two months, probably the shortest tour of any of the black field units. Many of the enlisted women were transferred to Fort Jackson, South Carolina, for assignment to the regional hospital there where they were in a position to earn technical ratings. The three commissioned officers had orders to report to Fort Des Moines, thus adding to the list of attached unassigned black officers there.[62]

One of the last black units to be activated during this period was the company at Camp Beale (California), organized in November 1946, and composed of some women transferred from Camp Stoneman (California) and Camp Atterbury (Indiana). Later, women from other stations were sent to Camp Beale. They worked at the separation center on the post where they served as clerks, clerk-typists, drivers, medical technicians, and in other positions for which they had army training or experience, such as food inspectors and photographers. Camp Beale and Camp Stoneman, along with Halloran General Hospital on Staten Island in New York and Lockbourne Army Air Base in Ohio, were the last four field locations for black WACs. At that time, there were 413 black enlisted women and 13 officers (some of whom had reenlisted) in the service.[63]

A black unit did not see overseas service until February 1945. Earlier efforts to send them overseas did not get off the ground. In late 1942, the European Theater of Operations (ETO) had requested black WACs for service in small units at locations near black troops. William H. Hastie, the first black civilian aide to the secretary of war, regarded the request as a disguised scheme to afford companionship for the soldiers. Hastie stated that the use of the women in this fashion was contrary to the announced purpose of the corps and would bring discredit to the organization. With Hastie's views in mind, the director of the corps, who had some misgivings about the plan, insisted on a unified command of the women at one location under WAC officers, whereupon the theater quickly canceled the request and made it clear that "colored [WAACs] will not be requisitioned until such time as the War Department announces that their shipment to theaters of operation is a necessity." In other words, the theater would have to be ordered by the War Department to request black women. In April 1943, the War Department, under pressure from black leaders, tried to activate a black shipping unit for overseas duty, but the ETO failed to send a table of organization—allocation of personnel, positions, and ranks and grades—for the unit. As late as June 10, 1943, the War Department notified the ETO that it had not received the table of organization for the shipping unit. Then on June 17, 1943, the theater canceled the request.[64]

In an attempt to assess black WAC interest in serving overseas, possibly to determine whether it was consistent with the demands of black leaders and organizations, some army officers and WAC staff solicited the women's views. Although not all of those asked wanted to go, the report sent to the assistant secretary of war by the advisory committee on special troop policies (which had inspectors visit "southern camps relative to racial matters") revealed significant interest in overseas duty. The report noted: "Negro WACs at most camps stated that they would like to have foreign service. They made the suggestion that WACs could be used as nurses' aides."[65]

Meantime, in view of public pressure, the War Department decided to send a black postal unit overseas, and it "directed" (army euphemism for "ordered") the ETO to requisition blacks. As early as September 1943, the War Department had received information from the Army Administration School, which offered a course in postal administration (the WAC Administration School apparently had no such course), that although some WACs had completed the postal administration course, none had been black. Despite the lack of training, and possibly because mail handling was regarded as an on-the-job training area, the War Department's Negro Troop Committee began to move on the project of filling the requisition for a postal unit. On December 14, 1944, the committee reported that 300 black WACs had been ordered to report to Fort Oglethorpe (Georgia) by January 15, 1945, for overseas processing and that an additional 500 would be sent in a later shipment.[66]

The Negro Troop Committee stated that it understood that the delay in getting the women out of the country was the failure of the European Theater of Operations to send specification numbers with the requisition—the failure to send a table of organization again. This problem caused some concern on the part of Colonel Hobby, who by this time had some question about the willingness of the European Theater to carry through on the project. Colonel Hobby wanted the women to go overseas once the War Department had approved of the plan. She sought and received support from General Styler.[67]

The ETO wanted additional grade allotments for the women, but the War Department refused this request. The women were, therefore, sent as overhead, which meant in part that they could expect no promotions except by attrition either within their own unit or the larger theater unit. The group at its welcoming ceremony was referred to as a "Casual WAC Detachment."[68]

The unit was designated the 6888th Central Postal Battalion and was the only black WAC unit to serve overseas during World War II. At its peak strength, the battalion consisted of 824 enlisted women and 31 officers, all of whom had volunteered for overseas service. It left the States in stages. Colonel Hobby traveled to Camp Shanks (New York) the embarkation center, to wish the first contingent of 500 women farewell as they embarked for England on February 3, 1945. Later, more than 300 left for overseas duty. The first group was greeted on its arrival in England by Brigadier General Benjamin O. Davis, Sr., then the highest-ranking black army officer, and Major Charity E. Adams, the battalion's commanding officer, whom the army had flown to England in January 1945.[69] The battalion remained overseas a little over a year, and was stationed in Birmingham in England, and Rouen and Paris in France, locations at which it cleared out mountains of undelivered mail.

On the eve of Memorial Day 1985, the *Washington Post* carried some remarks of Bessie L. Robinson, then an eighty-three-year-old resident of the United States Soldiers' and Airmen's Home in Washington, D.C. Robinson, who had enrolled in the WAAC in 1942 and retired in 1963 with the grade of sergeant major, was a member of the 6888th Central Postal Battalion. She said:

> I know for some Negroes, being in the Army at that time seemed to be difficult. But, for me, there are no sad

stories. . . . I had good assignments and dealt with intelligent people.

I was in Paris on V-E Day and that was a glorious time. . . . We danced through the streets with all the French soldiers. It was a day one would never forget.[70]

Other accounts of individuals in the unit attest to the high morale of the group, the tenacity it displayed in the performance of its duty, the leadership of its officers, and the goodwill of the English and French people. Perhaps the account of Margaret Y. Jackson, an enlisted woman in the unit, best sums up the work, the dedication to duty, and the spirit of the members of the 6888th. Jackson, who later received a Ph.D. in English from Cornell University and has since retired from university teaching, stated:

> When the unit arrived at a rambling old discarded boys' school in Birmingham, England, we were, after settling in our quarters, shown a gigantic auditorium with an extremely high ceiling. It contained nothing but mountains of mail and packages that almost touched the ceiling. Understandably, we were both appalled and intimidated by this extraordinary sight. Our orders were to redirect this mail, getting it to the ever-moving troops on the front lines and throughout the ETO. Of course, we realized the enormity of the task ahead of us: the necessity of re-establishing for thousands of constantly uprooted soldiers ties with their loved ones, relatives and friends. These ties, we felt, would strengthen their morale and, hence, improve the overall performance of their duties, whatever they were.[71]

Referring to herself and her WAC co-workers as "neophyte postal clerks," Jackson continued:

> As we labored at long tables, piled high with mail, we were more than objectively impressed by the stacks of letters which we sought to place into the hands of the individuals to whom they were sent. Many of these letters were from the same loved ones. . . . After weeks—even months—they finally wound up on the floor of the auditorium in the Central Postal Directory.

Many of us were as pleased as the soldiers must have been when stacks of letters were distributed to them at mail call. Not many people in this cynical age can fully comprehend our empathy with the troops we served, especially when we received word that particular service men on our rosters would never read the letters intended for them.[72]

Jackson wrote of the difficulty of the task:

Locating and redirecting letters and packages for thousands of troops in the ETO was not the seemingly easy task performed by workers in modern post offices. . . . Many of the letters were battered from constant redirection and were barely legible. Hundreds of packages, damaged by constant handling before our arrival, had to be repackaged and readdressed. Those of us who had never learned the art of professional packaging became experts.[73]

And yet, grade promotions were a rare commodity:

Like all other members of the armed services, we all wanted promotions in rank; however, we knew that they were not frequently awarded in service companies like ours. Though promotions were rare, I was rather early in our tour of duty promoted to the rank of sergeant (T/4), for what my supervisors humorously described as a monomaniacal dedication to duty.[74]

However, satisfaction and rewards came from a different source:

Our satisfaction—and rewards—came not only from seeing the mountains of mail dwindle to small hills but, more importantly, from listening to the words of the soldiers themselves. . . . Wherever we went after work hours [in Birmingham], particularly in long lines (queues) at the theaters, we were constantly approached by service men—singly and in groups—profusely thanking us for the packets of mail and packages that they had been expecting for weeks or months, but had received only after our arrival. These spontaneous expressions of gratitude were more than we had anticipated, but gave us even greater incentives to perform well our duties.[75]

Saying that they received similar expressions of appreciation from the soldiers in Rouen and Paris, Jackson then wrote about the unit's living and working accommodations:

> The bleak living conditions in the dilapidated school in Birmingham and in the sprawling old public building in Rouen did not dampen our enthusiasm. We had a keen sense of humor and became master improvisators. . . .
>
> In Paris, living conditions were greatly improved over those in Birmingham and Rouen. We occupied leading hotels in the heart of the city and ate army rations prepared by well-qualified French cooks. However, adverse working conditions reminded us that we were in the army. The large abandoned building that was transformed into a makeshift post office in Paris was equipped with primitive heating appliances. The hastily set up, continuously smoking stoves were actually a hazard to our health. Nevertheless, our work was performed as it would have been in an ideal environment. Most of the women whom I knew took these adverse conditions in stride, complained good-humoredly, and sought compensation in the cultural advantages that opened up to us on week-ends and vacations.[76]

Jackson mentioned "the genuine dedication to duty that prevailed throughout [their] period of service in the ETO" and stated that "sometimes against great odds, we carried out our orders and accomplished established goals."[77]

Reminiscing, Jackson wrote

> As I look back on my days in the service, I now realize that we were among the most courageous and adventurous of our contemporaries in America. We had voluntarily interrupted careers (many of us were students, teachers, or employees in safe government jobs) to tread unventured—and often dangerous—paths in an

auxiliary [later an integral part of an] army that was both sexually and racially segregated.[78]

Captain Abbie N. Campbell, the executive officer of the 6888th, stated that the women "did a fantastic job" and she was "real proud" of them. Campbell remarked that she "could not have worked with a more dedicated hard working group of women." She concluded, "I really enjoyed that tour better than any other" during "my whole time spent in the service."[79]

Although the unit set a record of handling 65,000 letters per work shift, or 130,000 in a sixteen-hour period, army postal and WAC staff inspectors reportedly were critical of the unit's efficiency. Without documentation, the official historian of the corps, purporting to quote in part from a report noted, "The WACs' [in the 6888th] performance was not entirely satisfactory to inspectors, who stated that 'production appeared to be low' and that 'girls relax on their jobs while mail accumulates.' " The army purposely retained in Europe one segment of the group whose "morale and efficiency were pronounced so 'exceptionally low' by a WAC inspector" in order not to give the impression that the unit was being returned to the States "under circumstances implying failure."[80]

The unit was praised for its military decorum, administrative proficiency, and especially its special service program, which, along with the recreational program, was directed by Captain Mildred E. D. Carter, a professional entertainer in civilian life. The unit was cited for winning the softball championship of northern France and the European Theater WAC basketball championship.[81]

Then tragedy befell the battalion. Three of the women died of injuries resulting from an automobile accident on July 8, 1945, in Neuville, France. Members of the battalion, not wanting the bodies of their comrades buried in body bags, chipped in and purchased coffins. The three, Pfc Mary H. Bankston of New York City, Pfc Mary J. Barlow of Hartford, Connecticut, and Sergeant Dolores M. Browne of Bridgeport, Connecticut, were buried in the American Cemetery, Omaha Beach, Normandy.[82]

The 6888th Central Postal Battalion was returned to the States in stages. The first group returned in November 1945 and the last group in March 1946. Major Charity E. Adams returned in December 1945 and at the separation center at Fort Bragg (North Carolina) prior to her discharge from the service, she was promoted to the rank of lieutenant colonel. After the departure of Adams, Captain Mary F. Kearney took over command of the unit. The unit's last commanding officer was Captain Bernice G. Henderson, who had previously been the battalion provost marshal. By December 5, 1945, there were 284 enlisted women and 14 officers in the unit. In February 1946 the size of the unit was reduced again.[83]

In her account of the unit, Margaret Y. Jackson wrote of the friendly reception the French and English gave them. She fondly remembered the teas some of them were invited to by the English. Bessie Robinson told of dancing in the streets of Paris with the French on V-E Day. Another member of the 6888th Central Postal Battalion said that the British treated them "beautifully." She added, "There were always invitations and parties to attend." The British, she recounted, went out of their way to welcome the members of the unit. She told of being in a London pub with some other black WACs and some British friends when some non-black American soldiers made some racially denigrating remarks. Their British friends, she stated, verbally took exception to the remarks. Major Adams also spoke of "the unkind statements and insults from our fellow American soldiers," who, she believed, "were the perpetrators of bigotry."[84]

At the fourth reunion of black WAACs/WACs held in Atlanta from October 3 to October 7, 1984, several women who had served with the 6888th talked of the difference in race relations in the United States and Europe. One said that the Europeans treated them like "royalty," whereas in the States they had to sit behind the engine and the coal car when riding on trains. She told a story of one of her experiences while traveling in England. She sought lodgings at an American Red Cross facility, but the Red Cross officials refused to put her up because they "did not want to offend Southern soldiers who were staying there."[85]

An article in the *Birmingham Sunday Mercury,* under the

caption "Things Talked About," may have expressed the sentiment and perception that the British had toward the WACs and that which the WACs had toward the British. The writer stated:

> A surprising fact concerning most of these WACs is that the nasal intonation characteristic of the speech of the vast majority of Americans is comparatively faint. They speak extremely good English—much better English than the average native. They have lively minds and an interest in historical England which is insatiable. They seem to know a great deal more about the Shakespeare country than most Midlanders.
>
> In fact, these WACs are very different from the coloured women portrayed on the films where they are usually either domestics of the old-retainer type or sloe-eyed sirens given to gaudiness of costume and eccentricity in dress. The WACs have dignity and a proper reserve.[86]

Speaking of Captain Mildred E. Carter, who was a professional entertainer in civilian life and whom the writer described as the welfare officer of the battalion, the writer related that she was "very eulogistic concerning the hospitality Birmingham is showering upon her charges." Expressing the group's appreciation, Captain Carter said, "I think everybody of prominence in the city has been to see us to give us a personal welcome." Carter added: "You have been very charming and we are indeed grateful. I should like particularly to thank the Birmingham Hospitality Committee; it is a large-hearted organization."[87] The writer of the article ended the commentary with the following statement, "I am delighted to be able to record that not once did I hear Captain Carter or her fellow-officers use the word 'Swell,' however enthusiastic they became about this or that."[88]

Mary McLeod Bethune and Colonel Westray B. Boyce, then director of the corps, were in New York City to welcome home the women who returned to the States in February 1946, but Colonel Boyce was displeased with the mode of return of the last segment of the unit. While waiting to be informed of the date of its arrival, she was "amazed to

note from a War Department press release" that the women
had arrived at Camp Kilmer ten days earlier. The director was
even more amazed to learn that the women were sent home
"in the hold of a ship," which she regarded as "undesirable
quarters for female personnel." She declared that seldom had
any WACs been required to travel in that manner, and then
only when shipping was tight. The director concluded that the
army was "extremely fortunate that thus far no serious
repercussions have come from the unfortunate occur-
rence."[89]

In the early part of December 1945, the corps itself had
asked the commanding general of the ETO to return all
personnel of the 6888th battalion to the States in January
1946, as "no suitable assignment will exist after Christmas
mail is processed" and as most of the women were eligible for
discharge from the service. The ETO commander replied that
he desired to retain the unit "until such time as personnel is
redeployed under redeployment policy."[90] No other available records indicate that the ETO had retained the women to
keep the public from getting the impression that they were
being returned "under circumstances implying failure." Since
the war was over, the corps wanted all of the women home in
January 1946, after the holiday mail was processed.[91]

As late as June 1946, both General Douglas MacArthur,
supreme allied commander of the forces in the Pacific
Theater, and General Joseph T. McNarney, commanding
general of the United States forces in the European Theater,
asked the War Department to send only non-black WACs to
their commands. When in mid-1946 black leaders wanted to
know why black women were not being sent overseas,
Colonel Boyce explained that the blacks remaining in the
service were mostly in hospital companies and that no
additional blacks were being recruited. When pressed further, Colonel Boyce offered the excuse of the nonexistence
of overseas housing facilities for black females. In truth, the
commanding generals of the United States overseas troops
did not want black WACs, and apparently some field commanders Stateside did not want or need them either.[92] At that
time, there were fewer than 600 blacks in the corps, compared to over 18,000 non-blacks. (See Appendix 2.)

Top: The 6888th Central Postal Battalion massing for a parade in Birmingham, England. *Bottom:* The 6888th participating in a V-E Day parade in England.

The 6888th Central Postal Battalion; the units at Gardiner General Hospital, Camp Maxey, Camp Atterbury, and Fort Dix; the companies at Douglas Army Air Field, Walla Walla, Fort McClellan, Fort Clark, Fort Knox, and Camp Breckenridge; most of the women at Camp Claiborne and Camp Forrest; and the detachments at Fort Benning, Fort Sheridan, Fort Riley, Fort Sam Houston, and Fort Huachuca—all (according to the assessment of the inspector general's observers, reports of army and WAC staff officers, and observations of reliable participants on location) rendered commendable service, some beyond the call of duty and some under difficult circumstances. The companies at Camp Claiborne and Camp Breckenridge need to be studied: the references to "bad attitudes" and being "race conscious" and showing "a lessening of the proper attitude by a minority group" may have issued from a desire on the part of the women to have been accorded a certain amount of respect. The women at Fort Devens had a field commander with a slavemaster mentality. Fuller accounts of some of these units may yet be written. Other units and individuals—those whose activities are unknown to this author—likewise are among the missing pages in the story of blacks in the Women's Army Corps who served during World War II. (For a list of black units in field assignments showing their location, their duties, and their commanding officers, see Appendix 5.) See the following pages for pictures of the women on the job in field assignments.

Commissary clerk.

Sheet metal worker.

Inspecting parachutes.

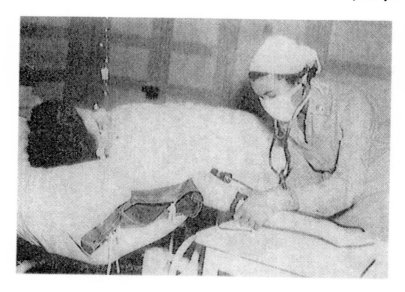

Top: Working at the base hospital in Walla Walla. *Bottom:* Transportation detail.

Top: Switchboard operators. *Bottom:* Quartermaster supply clerks.

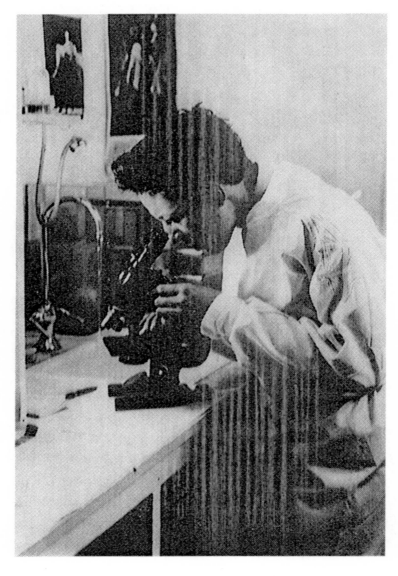

Laboratory technicians.

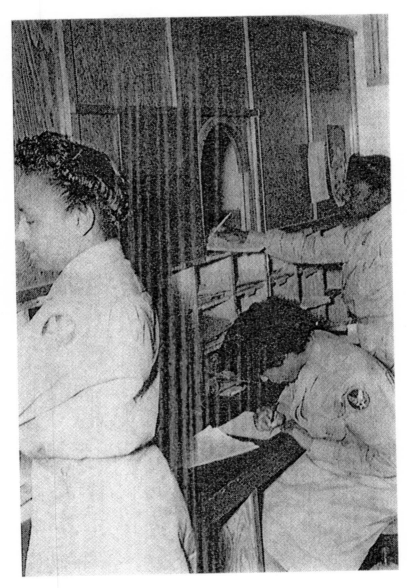

Message center.

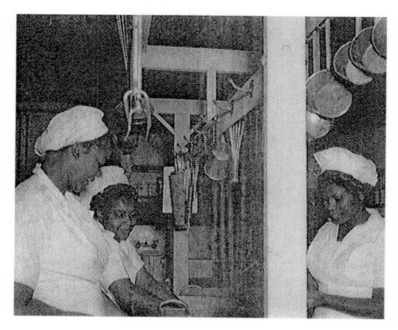

Top: Base files. *Bottom:* Mess personnel.

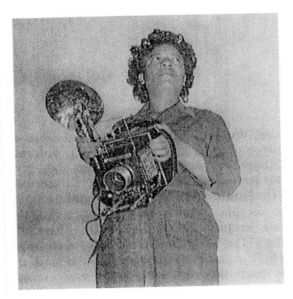

Top: Base photographer. *Bottom:* Assignments in the mimeograph section.

5. NOTES AND REFLECTIONS

Blacks in the Women's Army Corps were a cross-section of their civilian counterparts in their age group with the equivalent educational background. The women came mostly from urban areas and small towns and from all sections of the country. The Southerners among them outnumbered those from other sections. The overwhelming majority of them were in their twenties; the rest, except for a handful, were in their thirties. The vast majority of them were single. Some were married, some married after they entered the corps, some had been divorced, and some were mothers. The mothers among them either had children who were at least fourteen years old or had put their offspring out for adoption, usually with a relative. Most of the women prior to joining the corps had jobs, were looking for jobs, were in school, or were planning to continue their education.[1]

Many of the women had male relatives or friends in the service. Some had husbands who were servicemen, and a few had sons in the military. The fathers or male relatives of some had served in the Great War. Others had acquired some knowledge of the military; they were not totally ignorant of the structure of military life.[2]

All had enrolled with the expectation of doing something to help in the war effort, of doing something special and novel. They joined to serve. All had expected a fair shake within the framework of a segregated army. All had also expected some benefit from their service, some fulfillment of a cultural, social, educational, or economic nature. Most of them, if not all, had hoped the war would improve race relations in the nation; they were looking for a better social climate when the war was over. Before they entered they had heard the propaganda about the nation being the "arsenal of democracy," and once in the service during basic training they

Lieutenant Helen L. Cox weds Lieutenant Raymond Fleming at Tuskegee Army Air Base.

had seen the training films *The Four Freedoms* and *Why We Are Fighting*. They believed that the military would lead the way since it was fighting this war for democracy.

Enlisted Women

In retrospect, some of these expectations were too high— not because the women expected too much, but rather because the army, its policymakers, and some of its field commanders—the army was overwhelmingly Southern in its orientation and officer personnel—were too intent on running an apartheid-style operation. In pursuing this, the military failed to keep its pledge to many black WACs that it would not discriminate in job assignments and would accord them equal rights and privileges. In many instances, it made no attempt to ensure that its black personnel were accorded basic human rights in the Southern communities where they were stationed. It is doubtful that a more enlightened director of the corps could have changed things; the army was in control.

The army had too many field commanders like Colonel Crandall at Lovell General Hospital and Colonel Kelly at Camp Breckenridge who wanted blacks only to do the dirty work, and generals MacArthur and McNarney who did not want any blacks in their commands, and Colonel Throckmorton at Fort Knox who court-martialed the victims of a brutal off-post beating. It was only after persistent pressure from black leaders and organizations that the War Department ordered an unwilling European Theater commander, General Dwight D. Eisenhower, to request a black unit. Otherwise, the 6888th Central Postal Battalion, the only black unit that served overseas during this period, may never have existed.

Recruiting officers and press releases and news items had promised both black and non-black women who lacked military occupational specialities job training programs or on-the-job training. Yet in the early months of 1943, the corps stated that it had a serious problem: a large number of blacks whom it deemed "unassignable" with "no usable military skill." More than 900 blacks, almost one-third of the number of blacks then in the corps, were classified as unassignable.[3]

It appears that the bases for classifying these women as unassignable were their AGCT scores and their previous work experiences. In the early 1940s, both of these criteria were suspect as standards for determining what type of jobs blacks could do. In the first place, a large body of black Americans were woefully undereducated or miseducated, especially in the reputedly inferior dual school systems in the South, where a significant number of black WACs had lived. The corps knew (or should have known) that it was not going to get many of the better-qualified blacks because of its segregation policy. Further, American society had rigidly limited the job opportunities and hence the quality and quantity of the work experiences of its black second-class members.

Curiously, some of the eighty women in the Aircraft Warning Service whom the corps admitted to its first OCS class had low AGCT scores. The official historian of the WAC said of those women, "While the choices [made by the army air force] were later found to include some women without responsible paid experience and with test scores in the lowest aptitude category, Group V, the majority made successful officers."[4]

The corps, then, accepted non-blacks with low scores on the AGCT and commissioned them as officers and at the same time deemed black enlisted women with comparable scores on the test and comparable work experience as unassignable. This double standard was army policy. Henry L. Stimson, secretary of war, spelled out the intent of this policy when he noted in his Diary on March 12, 1942, that "the Army had adopted rigid requirements for literacy mainly to keep down the number of colored troops and this is reacting badly in preventing us from getting some very good illiterate [white] recruits from the southern mountain states." To bring in these "very good illiterate" non-blacks, Stimson endorsed a vigorous volunteer recruiting effort in the "southern mountain states."[5]

The WAAC had reimposed higher standards in April 1943, it had refused to accept a large number of blacks whom it regarded as unqualified, and it had withdrawn black recruiting officers from the field. About the same time, as of April 30, 1943, 645 blacks were on inactive duty awaiting orders to move to the training centers. Many of those whom the corps regarded as unassignable were sent to Fort Devens and then returned to Fort Des Moines when the training center at Fort Devens was closed. The noticeable decline in black enrollment at this time seems to indicate that some were discharged from the service at the convenience of the government. It appears, then, that the corps, in keeping with Stimson's policy, not only put a damper on black recruiting by raising standards but also got rid of some of those already in the service while it was conducting a vigorous recruiting campaign to bring in non-blacks.

At one point, in response to inquiries by black leaders, both the War Department and the commandant at Fort Des Moines asserted that blacks did not have the qualifications for (nor did test scores show they had the aptitude for) "specialized training in radio or other technical programs."[6] Assertions of this nature were incredulous in view of the presence of some highly talented enlisted black women in the corps—individuals who had scored in the upper groups on the AGCT, and who later went on to become commissioned officers and returned to civilian life to become doctors, dentists, lawyers, teachers, college professors, administrators, professional musicians, and social workers. These types of assertions also reveal something of the image that the army and society had of blacks and that dictated in large measure the type of specialized training they would get, their job assignments, their locations, their grades and ranks, and who among them would be discharged at the convenience of the government. In a word, this type of perception dictated in most instances how black women would be treated in the corps.

Very few, if any, of the enlisted women were sent to any of the specialized schools or took any of the technical courses except Cooks and Bakers School, Administration School, Motor Transport School, and Medical Technician School. Members of the 404th Army Service Forces Band took course work on their off-duty time at Drake University and not on temporary duty at the Army Music School. Members of the 6888th Central Postal Battalion got self-directed on-the-job training; they were not given the opportunity to attend the postal administration course at the Army Administration School. The corps even contended that some of the training programs that enlisted women were permitted to take were too difficult for blacks to assimilate. It said: "For Negroes only, the requirements for motor transport school were waived, and technical subjects removed from the course, but even with this assistance very few qualified drivers could be produced."[7] The record shows that, among others of equivalent talent, Juliette M. Simmons and Ethel E. Heywood were graduates of Motor Transport School before entering OCS and that at least two other black officers had completed the program at the Motor Transport Specialist School.[8] Surely it was not necessary to waive the requirements for all of the blacks who took the course, as the statement says.

About the same time that the army and the corps were

making these statements about the intellectual inadequacies of blacks, the chaplain at Fort Des Moines was writing to Truman K. Gibson, Jr., the civilian aide to the secretary of war, about how to get a black enlisted woman, Mona Washington, an assignment commensurate with her training and experience. Washington was a registered pharmacist, a graduate of Freedmen's Hospital in Washington, D.C., and a practicing pharmacist in her own drugstore. The chaplain's fears were realized when Mona Washington was shipped to Fort Dix (New Jersey), where at that time "quite a number" of women in her company were "working in the Station Hospital as permanent Mess Attendants," or kitchen police. Mona Washington was later shipped to Midland Army Air Base and, then, to Amarillo Army Air Base, both in Texas. It was only when she was stationed at the latter base that she received an assignment more compatible with her training and experience. A writer for the *Chicago Defender* suggested that the real reason for the small number of blacks who had training in specialist schools was that many of these schools were in the South and that black females were not wanted there.[9]

Many others in addition to Mona Washington and those in her company who were permanent kitchen police were malassigned or misassigned. There were some at Fort Sam Houston, those doing the "dirty work" at Lovell General Hospital, those at Camp Breckenridge working as laundry workers, hostesses, soda jerks, and sweepers in warehouses, and those at Fort McClellan working as maids in a civilian dormitory and waitresses in the officers mess. Of those women in the 6888th, it was said: "Some 11 percent of the detachment had cause for considering themselves mal-assigned; about 10 percent were typists and 1 percent were stenographers, and these were admittedly underutilized in a postal directory." The statement concluded: "Had not the segregation policy prevented, these could have been scattered through other WAC detachments where their skills could have been employed."[10]

The black WACs performed the types of assignments which the army permitted them to do. They were the company cadre. They were the mess attendants, ward attendants, ward orderlies, and the medical and surgical technicians. They were motor vehicle drivers, messengers, chauffeurs, postal clerks, parachute packers, supply aides, service club aides, chaplains' aides, laboratory aides, recruiting aides, typists, clerks, and cooks. A few were receptionists, telephone and teletype operators, motion picture projectionists, photographers, graphotype operators, band members, light automotive mechanics, aircraft maintenance aides, cartographers, buglers, physiotherapists, editors, and auditors. Few held skilled jobs; the vast majority held semiskilled jobs. An overwhelming number worked at one time or another in hospitals.

Many of the women performed their duties at several different army or army air force installations. Ana Aikens, over a period of two years, had assignments at Fort Clark, Camp Gruber, and Fort Sam Houston. Bessie Robinson, after completing Administration School at Fort Des Moines, had duty stations at Fort Custer, Fort Sheridan, and Fort Sam Houston before joining the 6888th Central Postal Battalion. Lorraine H. Lewis, after basic training at Fort Des Moines, served at Fort Devens, Camp Atterbury, Fort Custer, and Fort Lewis (Washington). Ethel M. Jackson, after Administration School at Fort Des Moines, was sent to Camp Gruber and then to Camp Swift (Texas) before being processed for overseas service with the 6888th. Clora Reese served at Fort Clark, Camp Claiborne, Camp Atterbury, Camp Swift, and Fort Sam Houston. Some of the women had only one duty station. Hattie Bell, who took her basic training at Fort Devens, was assigned to Halloran General Hospital (Staten Island, New York) for three years. And Queen-Esther Moore served at Fort Knox after taking her basic training at Fort Des Moines.[11]

The grades that the women held were a reflection not only of their assigned duties but also of the perception that the army had of women, especially of black women. The fact that a significant number of blacks served at two or more installations placed them in a position in which their field commanders could claim that the women were not under their commands long enough to have been evaluated for promotions. Then, too, many of the blacks were sent to the field as basics, without any specialized training. Some units went to the field as overhead or overstrength, which meant that the unit itself or the command to which it was attached had exceeded its table of organization—its alloted number of personnel, grades, ranks, and military occupational specialities. The records at the National Archives contain scattered references to promotions having been frozen in designated units, both black and non-black.

The army staff officer sent to Fort Des Moines in November 1942 to assess what some black officers regarded as "unnecessary prejudice," recommended among other things that the black enlisted women "be promoted to noncommissioned officers as soon as practicable." Charity E. Adams, then the senior black officer at Fort Des Moines and later the commanding officer of the 6888th Central Postal Battalion, stated that "we worked very hard to get the NCO grades in the Training Center and in the 6888th CPD and we had some degree of success." The hospital surgeon at Camp Forrest, where a black unit was stationed, asserted that he thought that WACs with superior ability should be given an opportunity to advance. In particular, he stated that Sergeant Theresa M. McDuffie, who was black, had "all the qualifications to be commissioned as a dietitian, except for the requirement of two years' training in a civilian hospital." He stated that "she should be given credit for her work in any Army hospital and be commissioned."[12]

As a result of the efforts of Adams and other unit commanders, every company had a first sergeant or acting first sergeant; if she held the grade of first sergeant in a black unit, she was in most instances the highest ranking noncommissioned officer in the company. The first black WAC to become a first sergeant was Margaret E. Charity of Richmond, Virginia. Charity, who was elevated to the grade of first sergeant in February 1943, was stationed at Fort Des Moines. She later was assigned to Camp Rucker (Alabama) and Fort Jackson (South Carolina). Some other first sergeants were Hazel Luby of Philadelphia, Pennsylvania, who was assigned to Fort Knox; Sylvia L. Cookman, who served at Fort Riley and at Gardiner General Hospital; Ann L. Covington, who at one time was stationed at Fort Custer; Anne L. Cotten, who was assigned to the unit at Fort Jackson in 1944; Marcella Goodwin, who was assigned at Fort Ord (California); and Cleopatra V. Daniels, who was a first sergeant of one of the companies of the 6888th.[13]

The "Strength of the Army" report for July 1, 1945, shows that the total enrollment in the corps as of June 1945 was 90,780. Of these, .64 percent held the grade of first sergeant or master sergeant, .70 percent were technical sergeants, 4.02 percent were staff sergeants or technicians third class, 12.81 percent were sergeants or technicians fourth class, 22.53 percent were corporals or technicians fifth class, 26.63 percent were privates first class, and 32.67 percent were privates. More than 59 percent of the women in the corps, then, fell into the lowest two grades and more than one-half of these (or almost one-third of the entire strength of the corps) were privates. These percentages in actual numbers represented 583 first sergeants or master sergeants, 638 technical sergeants, 3,644 staff sergeants or technicians third class, 11,632 sergeants or technicians fourth class, 20,449 corporals or technicians fifth class, 24,173 privates first class, and 29,661 privates. The number of first sergeants or master sergeants rose to 613 in August 1945, and the number of technical sergeants increased to 733 in September 1945. In August 1945 the actual number of women in all of the other grades increased except those in the lowest two grades, while the total enrollment was declining. Since these monthly reports do not show a racial breakdown and since unit rosters and payrolls for the years 1944–1946 have been destroyed according to schedule, it appears that the number of blacks among them cannot be ascertained, nor can a list of the names of the blacks in any of the grades be compiled.[14]

An examination of the rosters of two black units and of a list of 685 women of the 6888th Central Postal Battalion, however, will provide a profile of the grades that these women held. WAC Detachment No. 2, assigned to the Army Service Forces Regional Hospital at Fort Jackson (South Carolina) as of December 1944 had a complement of 124 enlisted women. The 9951st Technical Service Unit, Surgeon General's Office, was located at Fort Custer (Michigan) and evidently was assigned to Percy Jones General Hospital at

Fort Custer. This company had 86 enlisted women on its rolls, and apparently a significant number of its personnel had come from the Fifty-fifth WAC Hospital Detachment at Gardiner General Hospital after its deactivation in June 1946. The list of 685 women who were transferred in grade to the 6888th was dated March 1945 and contained the names of 14 women who were also on the roster of the detachment at Fort Jackson. Of the 895 different individuals on these three lists, .44 percent were first sergeants, .33 percent were technical sergeants, 1.78 percent were staff sergeants or technicians third class, 11.73 percent were sergeants or technicians fourth class, 24.24 percent were corporals or technicians fifth class, 25.47 percent were privates first class, and 34.41 percent were privates. In actual numbers, there were 4 first sergeants, 3 technical sergeants, 16 staff sergeants or technicians third class, 105 sergeants or technicians fourth class, 217 corporals or technicians fifth class, 228 privates first class, and 308 privates.[15]

Although these 895 women made up more than 22 percent of the peak number of black enlisted women in the corps, their percentage profile may not be a representative sample of the grades of other blacks. The units examined were not typical black companies. The 685 women of the 6888th consisted of a mere listing of individuals; they were not an organized unit; and they were designated as non-table of organization. There were among them only one first sergeant and one technical sergeant, the latter also appeared on the roster of the detachment at Fort Jackson. The two hospital companies were not typical hospital companies since some black hospital units were assigned to station or base hospitals, others to regional hospitals, and still others to general hospitals—all of which had different tables of organization. The unit at Fort Custer with 86 members had 2 first sergeants, one of whom was designated as unassigned. It also had 2 technical sergeants. Only 4 of its members were in the lowest two grades. As a unit, its personnel had a grade profile higher than that of the corps as a whole. The table of organization for a unit at a general hospital permitted personnel to hold grades no lower than technicians fifth class.[16]

It is evident, however, from the grade profile of the 895

blacks that none held the grade of master sergeant. The profile also seems to indicate that proportionally blacks held fewer of the top four grades; for the corps as a whole, .64 percent of the women were first sergeants or master sergeants, .70 percent were technical sergeants, 4.02 percent were staff sergeants or technicians third class, and 12.81 percent were sergeants or technicians fourth class, compared with .44 percent, .33 percent, 1.78 percent, and 11.73 percent, respectively, for blacks. Proportionally, also, it seems that more blacks were in the lowest grade: 32.67 percent for the corps as a whole, compared to 34.41 percent for blacks.

After peaking in December 1944, the number of black enlisted women in the corps began to decline. As noted previously, in addition to "forced" discharges and resignations, some left because they were disillusioned by jim crow practices or "dirty work" assignments. Others left because of health or family problems, marriage, or pregnancy. Reportedly, 11,402 women (including 465 officers) were discharged because of pregnancy at the approximate rate of 4 per 1,000 per month from July 1942 to December 1946. No racial breakdown on pregnancy is available. One specific case at Fort Des Moines, and maybe others elsewhere, baffled officials and others stationed there. In April 1943, a black enlisted woman, who had been in basic training less than two weeks, gave birth to a healthy child in the post hospital. The woman claimed that she was unaware of being pregnant, but in any event the physical examination when she entered active duty should have detected her condition. The army explained it away as a "careless" physical examination.[17] In reporting this incident to headquarters in Washington, the commandant at Fort Des Moines wrote, "As a sidelight, you might be interested to know 'Inky,' the little boy WAAC born at the station hospital." Colonel McCoskrie added, "I guess you can call all the WAACs in his company godmothers, as they all chipped in and bought the youngster a layette that was a knockout." McCoskrie stated that the female contract surgeon told him that the baby "is really a cute little fellow." He also indicated that photographers were barred, and that he had tried to keep publicity down. He concluded by saying that the mother of the baby would be discharged when the medical director released her from the hospital.[18]

The chipping-in to buy a layette for the baby and the chipping-in by the women in the 6888th to buy coffins for their fallen members seem to indicate that a camaraderie had existed among black enlisted women in the corps. On the other hand, it may have been this incident—the birth of a baby to an unwed mother—that led Major George Martin, the director of the WAAC control division who visited Fort Des Moines three weeks after the event, to assert that many black WACs "are of such inferior quality . . . in character." Such remarks reflected a common practice of non-blacks of condemning all blacks for the indiscretion of some.

Officers

Almost all of the black officers had some college education; several held advanced degrees. In the first class were graduates of Fisk University, Tuskegee Institute, Chicago Teachers College, Hampton Institute, Chicago Academy of Fine Arts, Kansas State College of Agriculture and Applied Science, Spelman College, Prairie View Agricultural and Industrial College, Indiana University, Bennett College, and other postsecondary schools. Those who were commissioned later held degrees from some of these schools and from others, such as Howard University, Virginia State College, Ohio State University, Wilberforce University, St. Augustine College, Kentucky State College, University of Chicago, University of Illinois, and Hunter College.[19]

They had been public school teachers, junior college teachers, four-year-college teachers, social workers, state and federal civil servants, dietitians, public relations professionals, and administrative assistants. One had had a successful career as a professional entertainer. Another was managing editor of a black newspaper. A third had been an evangelist with the African Methodist Episcopal Church and had been involved in extensive speaking engagements before church groups. A fourth was an assistant editor of a women's club magazine and had engaged in public relations work for the black women's club movement. A fifth had been a podiatrist. The majority had been trained as teachers, and many of these had had classroom experience.[20] (See Appendix 4 for a list of names of officers showing hometowns or places of enrollment.)

Before entering OCS, some had gone to Administration School or Motor Transport School or Cooks and Bakers School. After completing OCS, some had further training at Intermediate Officer School or Mess Officers School or Adjutant General School or Quartermaster School. Few, if any, were sent to the other army specialist schools. None went to the Command and General Staff School at Fort Leavenworth (Kansas), although non-black WAC officers were in school there.[21]

In January 1943, the War Department sent out by SOS a policy statement on the "assignment of Negro Officer Personnel" of the "Women's Army Auxiliary Corps." This statement rescinded an earlier one which was dated April 28, 1942. The January policy statement declared that black officers "will be assigned only to such type colored units and to installations and in such grades [in those positions] as are authorized by the War Department." The statement further specified that assignments of black officers were to be in the "following main categories: units to which Negro officers are not [now] assigned, units which are now activated but to which no Negro officers have been assigned, units not yet activated, and overhead positions." The statement made it very clear that "senior Negro officers will not be assigned to a unit having white officers of other arms and services in junior grades." The statement was sent to the commanding generals of all of the arms and services and base commanders with instructions to inform all commanders under them.[22]

It had been a common practice in the army for black units to have an all-non-black commissioned officer staff or an all-non-black cadre, and the WAC had such companies. This policy did not change that, but if a black officer were assigned to a black unit having non-black officers, this black officer would have to be a junior officer. More importantly, this policy statement rigidly limited the type of assignments open to black officers and restricted their upward mobility, since black units generally were no larger than companies whose

6th Co. 3rd Reg., first WAAC training center, Fort Des Moines, Iowa, May 29, 1943.

table of organization provided for a rank no higher than captain.

So, despite their many and varied skills, abilities, training, experiences, and activities, and despite Mary McLeod Bethune's continued concern about the type of assignment blacks should have, the overwhelming majority of the black officers became company cadre. Almost all of those withdrawn from recruiting were reassigned to company work; only a few escaped. Harriet M. West—one of the few—served briefly as "Negro advisor" at headquarters in Washington before being shifted to the adjutant general's office, where she apparently was not involved in or knowledgeable about policy or planning relative to blacks. A few other officers were recreational and special service officers. A few others worked in the quartermaster's corps. Mary L. Lewis, after a brief stint in food administration and food management, was consigned to company work at Fort Des Moines.[23]

Margaret E. Barnes, who was a personal secretary to her mother, a prominent civic leader, and was an assistant editor of a club magazine, and who in 1944 was the commanding officer of a black unit stationed at Staten Island, New York, was recommended to headquarters in Washington "if there is a need for someone to give special attention to public relations as they relate to Negro WACs." Barnes was described in the recommendation as "intelligent and experienced in public relations" and one who was believed to have done public relations work for the "Negro Women's Clubs." Barnes, it was felt, could do the job "if it is ever decided to add a Negro WAC to the WAC Group at the Pentagon." Barnes continued in company work. She did become the public relations officer of the 6888th, but she was still regarded as part of the unit's cadre.[24]

Vera Campbell, the podiatrist who prior to entering the corps was employed by the New York City Department of Welfare, was sure that the army, which traveled on its feet, could use someone with her specialty; she became and remained a company officer. The army's loss was the gain of the black officers' at Fort Des Moines; one of them remarked that they were fortunate because "we had a podiatrist in our group who kept our feet in good condition."[25]

Sight unseen, some field commanders questioned black WAC officers' ability to do company work. The commanding officer at Fort McClellan had expected non-black officers to have been sent with the black unit and was disappointed when he discovered an all-black cadre with the troops. However, once the unit became operational, he had to confess that he was satisfied with the black commanding officer.[26]

The army and the corps, fettered by their racist views that blacks did not have the aptitude or intelligence to engage in certain technical, administrative, statistical, and analytical jobs, wasted a lot of talent. Most importantly, they failed to utilize those blacks with training and teaching experience in the training center instructional programs, except in close-order infantry drill and calisthenics, which were the lot of most company cadre officers at the training centers.

The War Department policy statement of January 1943 virtually tied black officers to company work, and the Stimson formula (which was implemented by the corps in April 1943), joined with the established segregation policy, greatly limited the field of potential black recruits. Yet, as of October 1943, there were thirty-nine black officers stationed at Fort Des Moines—some were attached unassigned and some had recently returned from army schools or field assignments— more black officers than needed to staff the black basic training companies. This situation may have accounted for the assignment of a few blacks as junior officers in non-black or multiethnic special training units and opportunity school companies and in quartermaster supply. This situation also may have accounted for the admission of fewer blacks to OCS; for a whole year—from July 15, 1944, to July 21, 1945—no blacks were commissioned.[27] (See Appendix 3.)

Although thirty-five of the thirty-six black officers who graduated with the first class received promotions some four months after having been commissioned, and some of these same officers were promoted again later, black officers in subsequent classes did not fare so well. Apparently as a result of questions raised by black leaders about the slowness of promotions of black officers, all commanders were requested to report whether the individual black WAC officers in their commands were eligible for promotion under the time-in-grade requirement, whether they were qualified for promotion, and the reasons promotions had not been made.[28]

Of the thirty-nine black officers at Fort Des Moines, seven, (including five first lieutenants) who had been in grade six months or longer, were deemed not "qualified for" and not "deserving of promotion." The reasons that the post commander gave for this evaluation ranged from not having had an efficiency rating higher than "satisfactory" or "very satisfactory" to never having "served in an important position to justify recommending for promotion." Two other officers, one of whom had an excellent rating, had not been at Fort Des Moines long enough to get a rating there. The rest, the post commander stated, had not met the six-month time-in-grade requirement. At other installations, table of organization constraints were given as reasons for not promoting blacks.[29]

Three months later, the War Department rescinded its previous policy on promotion for black officers. Regulations were still to be followed "except that position vacancies will be created for them, as they become capable of duties and responsibilities of higher grades, by transfer of white officers to other units and installations." Black officers, however, "must be assigned to units composed of Negro enlisted personnel." This modification was made even though an officer who was executive officer of the WAC complained that 90.9 percent of the non-black second lieutenants had been in grade longer than three months, whereas only 70.4 percent of the black second lieutenants had been in grade longer than three months.[30] But percentages are not so meaningful when a comparison is made between a group of fewer than 100 and one of 5,000. Moreover, nothing was said about percentages and the actual number of these two groups of officers holding ranks higher than second lieutenants.

Six months after the policy modification—in August 1944—the NAACP complained about "the failure to promote" black "WAC officers in accordance with their records and ability, and a general unwillingness to afford opportunity to colored WACs for service comparable to those given to white WACs." The NAACP also noted that it had information "that some ten or more colored WAC officers who were commissioned one to two years ago and who have been kept in the pool of unassigned officers under Washington supervision at Des Moines are to be placed on the inactive list if a recommendation of Colonel McCoskrie is approved by the War Department." If this information was correct, the NAACP declared that the release from active duty of these officers "would be most regrettable in the light of the apparent unwillingness of certain officials of the Army to give colored WAC officers opportunity to serve their country."[31]

The War Department retained its low estimate of black officers' ability and capacity to meet the "responsibilities of higher grades." The table of organization for black units that then existed provided for an officer rank no higher than captain, yet many black company commanders held the rank of first lieutenant.[32]

Harriet M. West was "very much interested and very anxious . . . to go overseas" as commanding officer of the 6888th because she understood "that quite a large number [of enlisted women and officers] will be going that there is a possibility of an officer of field grade being sent." West wanted the job, at least in part because it would have provided an opportunity for promotion to lieutenant colonel (several non-blacks held the rank of lieutenant colonel including the person from whom West was seeking consideration). West did not get the assignment because she had had no troop experience, yet Charity E. Adams, who became the battalion commander, retained her rank of major throughout her tour of duty with the 6888th. It was not until she had returned to the States and was at the separation center being processed for discharge from the service that she was elevated to lieutenant colonel.[33] Promotion in rank on the eve of discharge was a courtesy in the army for those who probably should have been promoted while on active duty but who for some reason (such as the nature of the assignment, the table of organization, or late processing of records) did not receive it. In Adams's case, it appears that race precluded it.

Neither the concept nor the reality of fairness was operative in the corps, but neither was U.S. society's treatment of its blacks fair. In some respects, however, many blacks got a better deal in the WAC than society offered them in the civilian sector.

It was a lonely life for some of the black officers. The Futrell case pointed to their social isolation. Colonel Hobby was made aware of the problem when she reviewed the record of the case, yet, in discussing the lack of companionship for the few blacks in OCS at Fort Oglethorpe, she intimated in a less than apologetic manner that social isolation was one of the burdens they would have to endure.[34] Some learned firsthand what was meant by the Southern way of life and saw the ugly face of racism. Others observed the nature of race relations in the North and discerned some of the less virulent forms of racism.

Black officers and enlisted women served honorably and

loyally at a time of national crisis. Many of their talents and skills—actual and potential—were not desired and hence not utilized. But they served and had the satisfaction of knowing that they helped in the war effort and that they were among the pioneers in the Women's Army Corps. There were not many of them; they were under a quota system. However few they were, they and their fellow Afro-Americans in the other branches of the armed services and in the civilian defense industries were in a very real sense answering a call issued during World War I by the black intellectual and civil rights leader, W. E. B. DuBois, when he advised blacks, "Let us, while this war lasts, forget our special grievances and close ranks shoulder to shoulder with our white citizens and the allied nations that are fighting for democracy."[35]

Mildred C. Kelly, who enlisted in the corps in 1950 and who subsequently was appointed the first female sergeant major of the Aberdeen Proving Ground, in a tribute to those who went before, said at the opening session of the fifth reunion of Black WAAC/WAC and Women in the Service:

> My thanks to all of you who paved the way in the WAAC and made it possible for me and others to achieve goals that may not have been possible had you not accepted the challenge in 1942.[36]

Postscript

A few of the blacks, both enlisted women and officers, remained or reenrolled in the WAC. Most of these individuals, if they stayed in long enough, had the better fortune of serving in a desegregated army: an army not devoid of racism, but an army that provided more opportunities for blacks than existed during World War II.

Among the enlisted women who remained or reenrolled was Lorraine H. Lewis, who served from 1944 to 1958 and retired on disability from Walter Reed Army Hospital, in Washington. Bessie L. Robinson served continuously from 1943 to 1963 and was retired with a ceremony at Fort Meyers, Virginia, on March 31, 1963. Both Bertha M.

Parker, who stayed in for twenty years (from 1943 to 1963), and Catherine L. Bowie, who returned to civilian life in 1967, had continuous tours of duty.[37]

Some reentered after a break in service. Novella Auls, who enrolled in April 1943 and was discharged in November 1945, reenlisted in February 1950 and retired in July 1967. Auls had served during her first tour of duty at Fort Huachuca and overseas with the 6888th. Rachel Stewart Mitchell entered the corps in 1943 and was discharged in 1945; she reentered in 1948 and left the service in 1951 in the grade of first sergeant. Bertha C. Dupree, after serving with the 6888th, was discharged in December 1945. Dupree returned in November 1950 for a one-year tour of duty. And, Gurthalee Clark, a member of the black band, reenlisted in November 1946, after having been discharged in December 1945.[38]

Some enlisted women became officers after their reentry. Louise Bromfield, who entered the service in August 1944 and was with the 6888th, was appointed warrant officer, junior grade, in 1949 and chief warrant officer in 1953. Audrey E. Harris was an enlisted woman from 1944 to 1946 and was commissioned in April 1951. In the interval during her break in service, Harris earned a degree from Nasson College in Maine. By 1963, Harris had attained the rank of captain. And, Helen P. Hughes, who enrolled in the corps in 1944, was commissioned a second lieutenant in 1949.[39]

Among the officers, Bernice G. Henderson and Minnie P. Patterson were the first two black officers integrated into the regular army. Henderson, who was the commanding officer of the last segment of the 6888th, retired on January 31, 1959, apparently after a tour of uninterrupted service. Patterson, who had been discharged in April 1946, earned a master's degree from New York University in 1949, reentered the service, and resigned in February 1951. Ann G. Hall, who was separated from the service in January 1946, and Doris Norrel Williamison, who was separated in December 1945, were both recalled in September 1948 to serve at the WAC training center at Fort Lee, Virginia. Catherine G. Landry was discharged in October 1946 and reenrolled as an enlisted woman in 1947. In April 1947, Landry again was commissioned. Ruth A. Lucas, who entered the corps with the first OCS class, opted for the regular air force and was on active duty in 1963 as a lieutenant colonel.[40]

Margaret E. Barnes Jones, after her discharge from the corps, earned a degree from Howard University in 1947 and reentered the service. Before her retirement she served as a public relations officer. Jeanne C. Webster, likewise, earned a degree from Howard University and reenrolled. Jeanne G. Childs, who started her service as an auxiliary and attained the rank of captain, was assigned to the aural rehabilitation unit in the supply account section at Walter Reed Army Hospital. Childs retired from the service after twenty years. Harriet M. West remained in the corps until May 1952. After the war, West did get an overseas assignment: she was the assistant post inspector at Kitzingen, Germany. West, who had been promoted to major in August 1943, was still a major in 1948.[41]

Those who returned to civilian life carried with them an appreciation of the value of teamwork and an enhanced image of self, extremely important since they raised the sights of the women at a crucial period in the nation's history, a period which witnessed an ever-mounting demand for black respectability and civil rights at home and black nationhood in Africa and the Caribbean.

With their army job experiences and skills, joined with the G.I. Bill of Rights, which provided opportunities for career advancement and home ownership, and with veterans benefits, which offered preference for civil service jobs, reinstatement to their former jobs, and other advantages, these women no longer were satisfied to work as domestics or personal servants, which heretofore had been the source of livelihood of an overwhelming number of black women. These former WACs became a part of the vanguard of self-made women who went into the offices, hospitals, schools, colleges, state and federal civil service, and the professions. They became clerks, typists, auditors, nurses' aides, nurses, dietitians, teachers, personnel officers, social workers, doctors, dentists, lawyers, administrators, and members of the clergy. They became a part of the nucleus of an expanding black middle class.

Among the enlisted women, Margaret Y. Jackson, the T/4 in the 6888th, was a college and university professor before her retirement. Allie L. Davis, another member of the 6888th, who was a student at Langston College in Oklahoma before entering the corps, continued her education after returning to civilian life. She attended Savannah State College in Georgia, earned a master's degree from Southern Oklahoma State University, and did additional graduate study at the University of Illinois. After thirty-five years of teaching—most of it in Colbert, Oklahoma—Allie Davis retired in 1985. Willie M. Whiting, a native of Chicago and a private first class in the 6888th, earned a law degree from the John Marshall School of Law and practiced in Cook County, Illinois. Whiting later became a judge in the circuit court of Cook County. Clementine McConico Skinner, another native of Chicago and a member of the 404th Army Band, earned a doctorate and taught in the Chicago public school system before assuming an administrative post in that school system.[42]

Ethel M. Jackson, who had assignments at Camp Gruber and Camp Swift before joining the 6888th, received a degree in social work from Atlanta University in Georgia and pursued a career in social work until her retirement. Mary Ruth Harmon, a private first class in the corps, became a psychiatric social worker in Detroit, Michigan, her hometown. Patricia Shook from Nashville, Tennessee, became a dental surgeon and located her practice in Los Angeles, California. Mattie L. Edmond of Baton Rouge, Louisiana, who was a T/4 at the reception center at Fort Benning, took her postsecondary education at Southern University in Baton Rouge and moved to California, where she continued her education at the University of California and California State University. Edmond retired after a successful teaching career in the Los Angeles public school system. Clora Reese, who was stationed at Camp Clark, Camp Claiborne, and Camp Atterbury, became a recreational supervisor for the Department of Recreation and Parks of the City of Los Angeles. Reportedly, Reese also was employed as a radio and television announcer.[43]

Some former enlisted women worked in the public sector,

and some worked in the private sector. Virginia Lane of Minneapolis, Minnesota, who was assigned to the air force bases at Walla Walla and at Wendover Field (Utah) and to the 6888th, worked as an accountant for the federal government until her retirement in 1973. And Rosine Vance of Mount Vernon, New York, who was a T/4 in the Fifty-fifth WAC Hospital Company, worked for twenty-eight years at the Consolidated Edison Company in New York.[44]

Most of the former WACs mentioned above and some of the officers whose names appear below were enlisted women in the corps at the time the commanding officer at Fort Des Moines and the War Department claimed that none of the blacks had the qualifications or aptitude for training in army specialist schools.

Among the officers, Cornelia Bragman and Juliette M. Simmons completed medical school at Howard University. The latter, before entering the corps, was a resident of New Haven, Connecticut, and a teacher and social worker in Pike County, Alabama. Simmons graduated from Motor Transport School at Fort Des Moines prior to entering OCS. Ethel Heywood of Washington, D.C., also completed Motor Transport School before entering OCS. On her return to civilian life, Heywood worked in the federal civil service in Washington. Evelyn F. Greene, a resident of Washington and a member of the first OCS class, became a contact representative with the Veterans Administration in New York City. Oleta L. Crain, who had been commanding officer of a company at Camp Shanks (New York), became regional administrator for the Women's Bureau, Department of Labor in Denver, Colorado.[45]

Ernestine L. Woods, a resident of Stamford, Connecticut, and one of the commanding officers of the all-black band, completed her degree at Howard University and taught music in the public school system in the District of Columbia before relocating on the West Coast. Charity E. Adams earned a master's degree from Ohio State University and held a job as registration officer with the Veterans Administration in Cleveland. She later served as personnel officer at Tennessee A and I University in Nashville, and at Georgia State College in Savannah, and as employment and personal counselor with the Young Women's Christian Association in New York City. At this writing, she is a community volunteer and a board member of the Dayton (Ohio) Area Chapter, American Red Cross, and the Dayton Power and Light Company. Dovey Johnson Roundtree, the officer who "worked her hips off" on the recruiting circuit, spoke out against the proposed all-black basic training regiment at Fort Des Moines, who was dubbed "the walking NAACP" by the authorities at Fort Des Moines, earned a law degree from Howard University. She worked for a while as a claims adjudicator for the Veterans Administration, served as an attorney-advisor to the United States Department of Labor, and as a legal consultant to other government agencies in Washington. She has practiced law in the District of Columbia and has appeared before the Supreme Court of the United States. Johnson also attended the Howard University School of Religion and was ordained a minister in 1961 and is, at this writing, assistant pastor at the Allen Chapel African Methodist Episcopal Church in Washington. In 1979 Howard University Law School awarded her the Distinguished Alumna Award, and in 1981, the National Bar Association presented her the Certificate of Honor.[46]

Other enlisted women and officers went to technical schools, business schools, colleges, and universities. Most of them entered the job market after leaving the service or after completing their educational program. Many had outstanding careers. Moreover, many raised families and simultaneously pursued careers. At their reunions, they tell stories about their life and times in the WAC. Some of these stories, no doubt, include the disappointing experiences some had on field assignments in the South and the mountains of mail confronting the 6888th as it began its overseas tour of duty. Particularly, those at Camp Maxey in 1945 could recall working around-the-clock when tragedy descended on a nearby town, and those in the 6888th could remember joyfully celebrating V-E Day in the streets of Paris. At these reunions, they remember the tragic deaths of the three women in France and pay tribute to their sister WACs who have passed on.

6. *EPILOGUE*

The women who remained or reenlisted or enrolled for the first time in the corps after World War II found the war-born organization in limbo; its congressional authorization was due to expire on June 30, 1948, and its total strength was steadily declining. It was not until February 1946 that Pentagon officials, after mulling over several proposals for the corps's retention and after being spurred on by civilian women's organizations, decided to seek legislation to give permanent status to the corps by making it a component of the regular army and the regular army reserve. But another year was to pass before the Pentagon related to Congress the specific provisions it wanted in the enabling legislation.[1]

The proposed legislation, titled the Women's Armed Services Integration Act, encountered a rough time in the Armed Services Committee of the House of Representatives. Some members of the committee, who spoke of the opposition of unnamed field officers and soldiers to women in the military and of the fears of these men of being commanded by women, wanted to gut the bill. Representative Margaret Chase Smith, a member of the committee, refusing to accept anything less than that which the Pentagon had proposed, outmaneuvered those who wanted to weaken or kill the bill. The legislation cleared Congress and obtained presidential approval just eighteen days before the corps would have died a natural death with the expiration of its congressional authorization.[2]

Charles H. Houston, the noted civil rights lawyer, and Walter White had strongly objected to the bill because it contained no anti-segregation and anti-separate-units provisions. They were highly critical of what they regarded as Harriet West's and Mary McLeod Bethune's support of the bill and, implicitly, the War Department's segregation policy. White told Bethune that the "movement for the abolition of all segregation in the armed services is moving with considerable speed especially since the President's Committee on Civil Rights" had called "for the abolition of segregation." He added that it "would be an insult for women to be segregated when male members" of the military "were not." White then asked Bethune to urge the National Council of Negro Women to "hit hard" to get an anti-segregation clause in the impending legislation.[3] But the mood in the Congress and in the military, especially in the army, was not receptive to desegregation, and hence nothing came of these efforts. Moreover, the bill was under heavy fire in the Armed Services Committee, and the inclusion of an anti-segregation clause would have been an additional encumbrance.

President Harry S Truman, however, had taken the initiative in advancing the civil rights of those Americans who were denied opportunity. The presidential initiative was born out of the Cold War, with the independence of Greece and Turkey threatened and allied troops in Berlin harassed, with problem areas in other parts of Europe and the Middle East, with developments on the domestic scene including politics, and the demands of the civil rights activists. His committee on civil rights, appointed in 1946, produced a program "To Secure These Rights," which called for the elimination of segregation. About the same time, another presidential committee recommended the end of segregation and discrimination in education. And on July 26, 1948, Truman issued Executive Order 9981, which called for equal treatment and opportunity for blacks in the military.[4]

When Executive Order 9981 was issued, the military, especially the army, after several studies and reports on the utilization of black troops in the postwar period, and after presidential prodding, was still insisting on the quota system and segregation. The executive order and continued presidential prodding led to the creation of the President's Committee on Equality of Treatment and Opportunity, whose report was approved on March 1, 1950. In accordance with this report, the army announced that beginning in April 1950 enlistments were "opened to qualified applicants without regard to race or color."[5] The quota system was out. Segregation was out. Segregation was out in the military some four years before the Supreme Court ruling in *Brown v. Board of Education*. But like the Brown decision, the army's announcement did not bring an immediate end to segregation.

In the meantime, changes were occurring in the organizational structure of the military. The Department of Defense was created in 1947, and members of the WAC were permitted to opt for service either in the separate air force or in the army. The Women's Armed Services Integration Act had given women status in the regular army and the reserves, and in 1972 they were permitted to enroll in the Reserve Officers Training Corps. Then in 1978, the WAC itself was disestablished and its members were assigned or could enroll in all branches of the army and the air force. Already in 1970 the director of the corps, who had held the rank of colonel since the birth of the organization, had been elevated to the rank of a general officer and had under her supervision those women in the army and air force who formerly would have been identified as WAC.[6]

Demobilization was thinning the ranks of the corps, and uncertainty about its future led other women to leave; hence, the War Department authorized a reentry program for non-blacks in February 1946 and for blacks in August 1946 to keep the corps viable until its future was determined. The program was designed to induce those former WACs who more than met the minimal standards to return. Reportedly, some who wanted to return had difficulty at the recruiting stations, which were manned in most instances by servicemen. Two blacks who did reenter in 1947 were Vivian B. Honore and Catherine G. Landry. Landry, formerly an officer, reenrolled as an enlisted woman and was recommissioned in April 1947. Honore, formerly an enlisted woman, received a commission in April 1949. Many, many more were to reenlist.[7]

In October 1948, four months after the corps attained permanent status, a basic training program began at Fort Lee (Virginia), and the corps was back in the business of accepting and training raw recruits. The first black WAC company to take basic training at Fort Lee began it program on November 15, 1948. Its officers were Bernice G. Henderson, Doris M. Norrel, and Ann G. Hall. The last two had been recalled to active duty to serve at the training center. It appears that only three black officers served continuously in the army from the 1942–1945 period into the 1950s: Bernice G. Henderson, Harriet M. West, and Jeanne G. Childs. Alma O. Berry, like Norrel and Hall, had been recalled to active duty; she was sent to Fort Ord (California) to command a company that was stationed there.[8]

The corps sought to bring into its ranks women between the ages of eighteen and thirty-four who had some military occupational speciality or who had the potential of acquiring a skill. As inducements, it offered women technical training before assignment to jobs. It promised some their choice of location of initial assignment. It "glamorized" its uniform several times—an indication that it may have thought that style or fashion or chic appearance would aid in recruitment or the retention of those already in the service. In January 1952, it launched a big recruiting campaign and dispatched additional officers to the service commands to participate in the drive. It also formulated a program for recruiting at colleges and universities. But still the number of women in the corps remained relatively small; the corps acknowledged that its problem was a "shortage of enlistments." Even its officer strength was some 7 percent below its authorization in June 1954.[9]

Shortages existed in both black and non-black recruitment. For example, a requisition from the European command in February 1949 for a detachment of fifty black WACs could not be filled "prior to 30 June 1949 due to small NEW [Negro enlisted women] strength, inability of rectg stas [recruiting stations] to meet NEW rectg figures, and recent policy that enlisted women must serve 6 mos [months] in the ZI [zone of interior, meaning the United States] before being eligible for o/s [overseas]." The corps, however, promised to send twenty-four black enlisted women and one black officer in October 1949, and an additional group to bring the total to fifty enlisted women sometime before June 30, 1950. Each of the twenty-four women who were sent to the European command before June 30, 1949, had a listed military occupational speciality number.[10]

The number of the women in the corps declined rather

sharply between February 1946 and June 1949. The total strength of the corps stood at 29,801 in February 1946 but dropped to 17,896 in June 1946, to 8,134 in June 1947, to 5,352 in June 1948, and to 4,909 in June 1949. The blacks among them numbered 673 in June 1946, 319 in June 1947, 125 in June 1948, and 352 in June 1949.[11] Much, if not all, of the loss in membership at least through June 1948 was due to the demobilization of those who had entered the service before the end of the war, the uncertainty on the part of some about whether the corps was going to continue in operation, and the virtual closing down of recruiting operation for new members while the corps was in limbo. The increase in the number of blacks in the corps in 1949 was due to those returning through the reentry program and those entering the corps for the first time after the organization resumed its recruiting operations. In view of the prevailing state of race relations in the nation, blacks were more likely to remain in the service, if given a choice, and to seek entry.

The number of WACs, both black and non-black, increased significantly during the Korean War period (1950–53) and the Vietnam War period (1961–73). Between these two wars, however, the corps lost 2,100, including 300 blacks. But from 1973 to 1984, membership in the corps increased each year to a total of 72,250. Black enrollment rose from 3,188 in 1973 to 14,688 in 1978, an almost fivefold increase over a five-year period, or from 19.9 percent of the total strength of the corps to 27.7 percent of all of the women in the organization.[12] (See Appendix 6.)

The increase in the strength of the corps from 1972 to 1984 may be explained by the entry of a significant number of younger women seeking to avail themselves of the educational benefits offered by the military or to buy time before making a decision on their future. The statements of two black enlisted women who served after the corps was integrated seem to confirm this conclusion. One, who was a master sergeant when she retired, remarked, "Sometimes I think that career women in the Army will become a thing of the past." She added that "there were hardly any women NCOs" in the upper grades when she retired. She concluded with the statement, "It seems to me that women aren't staying in long enough to make rank." The other woman said that she thought that "many women, like the men, come in while they make up their mind about what they want in life."[13]

Responding to a question of why she joined the postwar WAC, one black enlisted woman, who enrolled in 1960, stated that she wanted to serve as a medical technician; she explained that she had taken a prenursing course in high school. Once in, however, she was sent to a specialist school and was assigned as a communication specialist and later as an administration specialist. In addition to wanting to be a medical technician when she joined, this enlisted women said that the other attractions were "education, travel and excitement." She retired some twenty-five years after her entry "with no regrets."[14]

Another black enlisted woman, who advanced to the position of command sergeant major of a large army installation, stated that she had been a secondary school teacher but realized that teaching was the wrong career for her. "I went in the service," she said, "with intentions of staying one tour [three years], saving money and returning to grad school." After basic training at Fort Lee, she took the army clerical course and a course in leadership. Her three-year tour ended in the midst of the Korean War, but after a one-year extension during which she took some graduate school courses, she decided to reenlist and make a career in the army. She spent three years in Japan and volunteered to go to Vietnam several times, but the allotment for WACs was filled each time. In assessing her career in the WAC, she stated, "The Army was good to and for me," but, she declared, "I had to work hard." From the vantage point of 1986, she said: "Today if I was asked to pursue a career in the service I might not readily accept the idea. In view of the many job opportunities open to blacks and women in private industry as compared to the fifties, I just might say no thank you."[15]

After finishing college and working eight years in the personnel office of the black college which had granted her degree, a retired officer, who joined in 1958, said that she was "attracted to the military because of its policy on equal opportunity for jobs, pay, [and] rank." She, like others, stated that she "never intended to make a career of it." Receiving a

direct commission on entry, she took the WAC Officer Basic
Course and subsequently the Military Personnel Officer
Course and the WAC Officer Advance Course. Her first
assignment in the military was as an instructor at Fort
McClellan (Alabama), where a new WAC center and school
had been located since 1954. After twenty years in the WAC
with assignments as a company officer, personnel officer,
family housing officer in Germany, and executive officer to
the commander of the WAC center, this officer retired with
the rank of colonel on August 31, 1979.[16]

When asked why she stayed in the corps after her World
War II tour of duty, an officer responded with one short
sentence: "It was a job." She went on to explain that jobs on
the outside with comparable responsibility, pay, challenge,
and retirement benefits were hard to obtain in the 1940s. Her
postwar service was as the officer in charge of a base
publication office, where she supervised seven non-
commissioned officers—both WAC and army—and as a
company commander of a black WAC company. When this
company later had non-blacks added to its ranks, she became
the executive officer of the unit even though she outranked
the non-black commanding officer. Her reaction to the
situation was, "I was very angry, but there wasn't anything I
could do about it."[17]

Unlike those who served during World War II, they were
admitted to army technical schools and received training in
many military occupational specialities. They were trained as
photographers, occupational and rehabilitation therapists,
intelligence analysts, personnel administration specialists,
management specialists, communication specialists, motor
vehicle specialists, and military police training specialists.
Some of them worked on the same type of assignments as
those who went before. Most, if not all, of them had military
occupational specialities before being assigned to jobs. Nu-
merically and proportionally, more of them held higher
non-commissioned officer grades (including the grade of
sergeant major) and were assigned to more responsible jobs.
Mildred Kelly worked at the Pentagon for two years in the
grade of sergeant major before being transferred to Aberdeen Proving Ground where she became command sergeant

major, the first female command sergeant major of a large installation.[18]

The officers, likewise, had technical and administrative training and held more responsible (and a greater variety of) assignments. For example, Vashti V. Jefferies went to Command and General Staff School in 1963, the first black WAC to do so. In 1949, Louise B. Jones was appointed warrant officer and served as a warrant officer for three years; it was not until 1962 that another black WAC was appointed warrant officer. After serving in a variety of assignments in the Adjutant General's Corps, Eunice M. Wright at the time of her retirement was executive officer to the commanding officer of the WAC Center at Fort McClellan.[19]

They went overseas; they served in West Germany, Korea, Japan, Hawaii, and Vietnam. WACs went to Vietnam in 1965; blacks made up about one-third of a detachment of WACs who volunteered to go to Vietnam. The members of this unit were sent by the army to serve as medical technicians and to work in supply and administrative support jobs. Among those in this detachment was Ethel M. Dial, who was in charge of a group of Teletype workers. Dial, who retired from the service as master sergeant, recalled working twelve-hour stints and six-day weeks. Chief Warrant Officer Doris I. Allen served several tours of duty in Vietnam as a military intelligence analyst. Other blacks volunteered to go to Vietnam, some several times. But the army had only a limited number of positions there open for WACs. Those in Vietnam were not stationed in the immediate combat area. Blacks were in Vietnam as late as 1972; some had volunteered to extend their tours of duty and others came as replacements. Those who served in West Germany, Japan, and Korea usually stayed at their overseas posts for the full three-year tour of duty.[20]

Pushed by a combination of forces, the army grudgingly had relinquished its quota system and segregation policy. Yet at the WAC basic training center in Fort Lee (Virginia), blacks, although "integrated" in 1950, still lived in separated barracks. Blacks who were stationed in Japan in 1954 likewise lived in separate barracks. Curiously, the first instance of desegregation in the WAC occurred on foreign soil; in

December 1950, blacks who were stationed in Europe began serving in racially mixed units. The army dragged its feet; field commanders dragged their feet. Eventually, some field commanders began to assign or permit the assigning of women in their commands to barracks alphabetically.[21]

When asked whether blacks in the corps were still experiencing racial bias, discrimination, or denigrating incidents, one former WAC replied, "I was not at any time discriminated against as an individual, but we as blacks were." She added, "Knowing this to be a fact meant that I had to push harder [to get ahead], and I did." Another recalled only one incident which, she said, occurred at Fort Sheridan (Illinois). This former WAC related that a non-black officer from Mississippi told her that "she wasn't used to being around blacks" and sought to have the black WAC NCO reassigned. Instead, the officer was reassigned.[22]

A WAC officer who retired in 1979 stated that "race relations in the Army were good, or at least programs were in effect to work toward that end." She added, "I never felt that I was discriminated against in the Army because of my race, though I received complaints from other Blacks," referring to those in the lower ranks or grades. She acknowledged, however, that "discrimination was there, though subtle," and that she may have been spared from it because of her rank. But her rank provided no shield against the discrimination she suffered off-post in Alabama. The situation in Alabama, especially during the civil rights struggle in the 1950s and early 1960s, was so racially charged that she was relieved when an assignment took her to Germany.[23]

The post-World War II WACs, both black and non-black, were affected by the winds of change that swept across the nation and the world. The march of events affected all aspects of American life, including the military. The army was forced to compete on a different playing field, hence it made more opportunities available to blacks and improved their condition of life in the service. But as late as 1988, the annual report of the Defense Advisory Committee on Women in the Service stated that women and minorities were still exposed to "subtle and not-so-subtle harassment." The committee found that women still had to deal with job discrimination and that some military men were still unwilling to accept them in leadership positions. The committee also found that the race issue was still a problem in the military.[24] Blacks in the WAC from the very beginning were confronted with the twin problems of racism and sexism, and more than forty-five years later, although much has been done in opening the doors of opportunity, black females in the army, as in American society at large, still are confronted with the vestiges of racism and sexism.

APPENDIXES

Appendix 1. Officers Assigned to Recruiting

Initial Assignments, 1942

Names	Locations*
Mildred Carter	Boston, Massachusetts
Elizabeth C. Hampton and Verneal M. Austin	New York, New York
Evelyn F. Greene	Baltimore, Maryland
Ina M. McFadden	Military District of Washington, D.C.
Dovey M. Johnson and Ruth A. Lucas	Atlanta, Georgia
Doris M. Norrel and Glendora Moore	Columbus, Ohio
Mary A. Bordeaux and Gertrude J. Peebles	Chicago, Illinois
Charline J. May	Omaha, Nebraska
Alice M. Jones and Mary L. Miller	Dallas, Texas
Harriette B. White	Salt Lake City, Utah

*Some officers recruited throughout the area of the assigned service command; others worked out of several service commands. All were reassigned before the end of July 1943. Data taken from an undated memorandum in WAC historical file RG 165; papers in the Bethune Archives; and newspaper file at the Moorland-Spingarn Research Center.

Subsequent Assignments, 1943

Ruth L. Freeman   Recruiting and Induction
                       Station No. 2, Chicago, Illinois

Ethel E. Heywood   Recruiting and Induction
                       District, Syracuse, New York

Mary A. Moore   Recruiting and Induction
                       District, Newark, New Jersey

Mildred L. Osby   Military District of Washington, D.C.

Blanche L. Scott   Richmond, Virginia

Vashti B. Tonkins   Salt Lake City, Utah

Thelma B. Brown   Atlanta, Georgia

Katherine J. Hunter   St. Louis, Missouri

Appendix 2. Number and Percentage of Blacks in the WAAC/WAC, 1942–1946

Month & Year	Total	Total Officers*	Number of Blacks Enrolled			Percentage of Blacks Enrolled		
			Total	Officers	Women	Total	Officers	Women
Dec. 1942	12,767	1,545	220	59	161	1.7	3.8	1.4
Mar. 1943	44,530	2,501	2,532	65	2,467	5.7	2.6	5.8
June 1943	60,243	4,917	3,161	105	3,056	5.2	2.1	5.5
Sept. 1943	51,268	5,430	3,012	105	2,907	5.9	1.9	6.3
Dec. 1943	57,731	5,856	2,805	103	2,702	4.9	1.8	5.4
Mar. 1944	67,215	5,841	3,175	115	3,060	4.7	2.0	5.0
June 1944	77,152	5,855	3,506	117	3,389	4.5	2.0	4.7
Sept. 1944	86,351	5,930	3,766	121	3,645	4.4	2.0	4.5
Dec. 1944	90,191	5,852	4,040	120	3,920	4.5	2.0	4.7
Mar. 1945	96,859	5,795	3,902	115	3,787	4.1	2.0	4.1
June 1945	96,557	5,733	3,849	117	3,732	4.0	2.0	4.1
Sept. 1945	86,541	5,694	3,738	105	3,633	4.3	1.9	4.5
Dec. 1945	43,813	4,682	1,690	80	1,610	3.9	1.8	4.1
Mar. 1946	26,263	2,763	786	32	754	3.0	1.2	3.2
June 1946	18,510	1,793	673	15	658	3.6	.9	3.9
Sept. 1946	13,773	1,361	279	15	264	2.0	1.1	2.1
Dec. 1946	9,655	1,189	372	9	363	3.9	.8	4.3

*Excluding warrant officers. The number of warrant officers—there were no blacks among them—at stated periods were:

Mar. 1944	4	Dec. 1944	26	Sept. 1945	60	June 1946	18
June 1944	10	Mar. 1945	27	Dec. 1945	27	Sept. 1946	8
Sept. 1944	20	June 1945	44	Mar. 1946	26	Dec. 1946	5

Data taken from "Summary of Information on Negro Women Who Have Served or Are Serving in the Women's Army Corps, 1942–1963," prepared by the Division of Doctrine and Literature, United States Women's Army Corps School (1963). Data in this table appear in Tables I and II in Appendix A of Treadwell, *Women's Army Corps* (1954). The information from both of these sources appears to have been taken from the War Department mimeographed monthly "Strength of the Army" reports, copies of which may be found in the Center of Military History in Washington, D.C.

Appendix 3. Number of Blacks and Their Officer Candidate School Classes

Class	Total Enrolled	Failed, Resigned, or Had Health Problems	Number Commissioned	Date of Commission
1	41	2	39	Aug. 29, 1942
11	4	2	2	Jan. 9, 1943
12	8	2	6	Jan. 23, 1943
13	3		3	Jan. 30, 1943
14	1		1	Feb. 9, 1943
15	3	2	1	Feb. 16, 1943
20	2		2	Mar. 30, 1943
22	2		2	Apr. 10, 1943
23	3		3	Apr. 17, 1943
28	15	3	12	May 17, 1943
29	5	2	3	May 24, 1943
30	9	2	7	May 31, 1943
31	14	3	11	June 5, 1943
33	3		3	June 23, 1943
34	3		3	June 30, 1943
35	5		5	July 7, 1943
36	4		4	July 14, 1943
39	2		2	Aug. 13, 1943
40	1		1	Sept. 2, 1943
41	2	1	1	Sept. 18, 1943
42	6		6	Oct. 16, 1943
44	2	1	1	Nov. 6, 1943
46	8	2	6	Dec. 11, 1943
47	8	3	5	Dec. 28, 1943
49	3		3	Mar. 18, 1944
50	5		5	May 20, 1944
51	2		2	June 17, 1944
52	2		2	July 15, 1944
58	3		3	July 21, 1945
59	2		2	Aug. 8, 1945
60	1	1		Nov. 17, 1945
Totals	172	26	146	

Data taken from Lavinia L. Redd, "History of Military Training, WAAC/WAC, Army Service," pp. 259–60, 270–71. Redd's unpublished paper may be found at the Center of Military History, Washington, D.C.

Appendix 4. Black Commissioned Officers, 1942–1945

Members of the First Officer Candidate School Class
(Commissioned on August 29, 1942)

Name	Army Serial Number	Home
Charity E. Adams (Charity E. Earley)*	L 500 001	Columbia, South Carolina
Frances C. Alexander (Frances A. Futrell)	L 500 021	Toledo, Ohio
Myrtle E. Anderson	L 400 502	Kansas City, Missouri
Violet W. Askins	L 600 015	Chicago, Illinois
Verneal M. Austin	L 200 001	New York, New York
Mary A. Bordeaux	L 500 023	Louisville, Kentucky
Geraldine G. Bright (Geraldine G. Walker)	L 802 008	Pittsburg, Texas
Annie L. Brown (Annie Pendergraff)	L 801 508	Houston, Texas
Abbie N. Campbell (Noel C. Mitchell)	L 402 518	Tuskegee, Alabama
Vera G. Campbell	L 200 003	New York, New York
Mildred E. D. Carter	L 115 021	Boston, Massachusetts
Irma J. Cayton (Irma J. Wertz)	L 600 017	Chicago, Illinois
Natalie F. Donaldson	L 903 005	New York, New York
Sarah E. Emmert (Sarah E. Jackson)	L 600 018	Chicago, Illinois

*Names in parentheses denote known changes by reason of marriage.

Name	Army Serial Number	Home
Geneva V. Ferguson (Geneva V. Bland)	L 501 003	Camp Dennison, Ohio
Ruth L. Freeman	L 801 509	Liberty, Texas
Evelyn F. Greene	L 303 500	Washington, D.C.
Elizabeth C. Hampton	L 900 055	Los Angeles, California
Vera A. Harrison	L 500 024	Wilberforce, Ohio
Dovey M. Johnson (Dovey J. Roundtree)	L 308 002	Richmond, Virginia
Alice M. Jones	L 403 002	Nacogdoches, Texas
Mary F. Kearney	L 125 005	Bridgeport, Connecticut
Mary L. Lewis	L 400 501	Orlando, Florida
Ruth A. Lucas	L 125 004	Stamford, Connecticut
Charline J. May	L 703 003	Falls City, Nebraska
Ina M. McFadden	L 700 008	St. Louis, Missouri
Mary L. Miller	L 801 002	New Orleans, Louisiana
Glendora Moore	L 200 016	New York, New York
Sarah E. Murphy	L 402 005	Atlanta, Georgia
Doris M. Norrel (Doris N. Williamson)	L 500 022	Indianapolis, Indiana
Mildred L. Osby	L 600 016	Chicago, Illinois
Gertrude J. Peebles	L 703 002	Omaha, Nebraska
Corrie S. Sherard	L 402 006	Atlanta, Georgia
Jessie L. Ward	L 200 625	New York, New York

Name	Army Serial Number	Home
Harriet M. West (Harriet M. Waddy)	L 303 506	Washington, D.C.
Harriette B. White	L 900 054	Los Angeles, California

Data taken from *Philadelphia Tribune,* September 5, 1942; *Baltimore Afro-American,* September 5, 1942; and "Summary of Information on Negro Women Who Have Served or Are Serving in the Women's Army Corps," prepared by the Division of Doctrine and Literature of the United States Women's Army Corps (1963).

*Officers Commissioned in Subsequent Classes**

Name	Army Serial Number	Class and Year	Home
Margaret E. Allen (Margaret A. Smith)	L 200 135	30th, 1943	New York, New York
Pauline Atkins	Unknown	Unknown	Unknown
Margaret E. Barnes (Margaret E. Jones)	L 500 995	12th, 1943	Oberlin, Ohio
Margaret J. Barnes (Margaret J. Crawford)	L 600 722	Unknown	Kalamazoo, Michigan
Alma O. Berry	L 802 083	12th, 1943	Terrell, Texas
Consuelo Bland	Unknown	50th, 1944	Unknown
Cornelia T. Brangman	L 303 577	Unknown	Unknown
Josephine Brown	L 203 362	Unknown	Unknown
Thelma B. Brown	L 402 115	13th, 1943	Quitman, Georgia
Ruth E. Caldwell	L 401 046	Unknown	Orangeburg, South Carolina
Opal G. Campbell	L 502 057	34th, 1943	Center Point, Indiana

*From available data.

Name	Army Serial Number	Class and Year	Home
Virginia M. Cheeks	L 599 052	11th, 1943	Charles Town, West Virginia
Willia G. Cherry	L 600 718	12th, 1943	Detroit, Michigan
Jeanne G. Childs	L 501 178	Unknown	Unknown
Ann M. Clark	Unknown	15th, 1943	Lawrenceburg, Kentucky
Vivian M. Corbett	Unknown	Unknown	Unknown
Helen Louise Cox	Unknown	Unknown	San Mateo, California
Hazel E. Craddock	L 702 372	46th, 1943	Des Moines, Iowa
Oleta L. Crain	L 705 066	Unknown	Denver, Colorado
Florence M. Croner	Unknown	Unknown	Unknown
Edna Cunningham	L 900 406	Unknown	Unknown
Margaret A. Curtis	L 800 033	30th, 1943	San Antonio, Texas
Lillian Duncan	L 402 584	Unknown	Talladega, Alabama
Mildred D. Dupee	L 500 418	12th, 1943	Detroit, Michigan
Alice E. Edwards	L 900 401	31st, 1943	Los Angeles, California
Bertie M. Edwards	L 204 945	42nd, 1943	Danville, Virginia
Evelyn M. Edwards	L 402 536	28th, 1943	Tuscaloosa, Alabama
Thelma Edwards	Unknown	30th, 1943	Atlanta, Georgia
Vivian N. Elzie	L 304 676	Unknown	Unknown
Ermane S. Faulk	L 304 838	Unknown	Brooklyn, New York

Name	Army Serial Number	Class and Year	Home
Frances E. Flatts	L 201 378	28th, 1943	New York, New York
Ellsworth W. Fouche	L 401 048	Unknown	Columbia, South Carolina
Lois Freeman	Unknown	Unknown	Unknown
Catherine F. Gaines	L1 000 406	Unknown	Unknown
Stella G. Garvin	L 203 142	Unknown	Unknown
Catherine Godfrey	L 402 631	Unknown	Unknown
Gladys Gould	Unknown	Unknown	Unknown
Fannie A. Griffin	L 200 109	Unknown	Unknown
Patricia S. Gunter	L 403 194	34th, 1943	Nashville, Tennessee
Ann G. Hall	L 605 125	35th, 1943	Chicago, Illinois
Faricita Hall	L 303 954	28th, 1943	Berkeley, California
Aurelia Harris	L 701 068	Unknown	Unknown
Bernice G. Henderson (Bernice G. Hughes)	L 500 504	28th, 1943	Xenia, Ohio
Grace L. Howell	L 708 015	46th, 1943	Unknown
Ethel E. Heywood Ethel M. Smith)	L 302 035	11th, 1943	Washington, D.C.
Verdia M. Hickambottom	L 412 034	35th, 1943	Pasadena, California
Vera Hoddrick	Unknown	Unknown	Unknown
L. Hoskins	L 801 779	Unknown	Unknown

Name	Army Serial Number	Class and Year	Home
Katherine J. Hunter	L 401 523	15th, 1943	Tougaloo, Mississippi
Ethel M. Jackson	L 409 029	Unknown	Unknown
Lacy Johnson	L 800 584	30th, 1943	Unknown
Victoria G. Jones (Victoria J. Poole)	L 801 186	13th, 1943	New Orleans, Louisiana
Merceedees A. Jordan	L 200 271	30th, 1943	Belmar, New Jersey
Catherine G. Landry	L 303 726	28th, 1943	New Orleans, Louisiana
El Freda Le Beau	L 801 480	Unknown	New Orleans, Louisiana
Marguerite L. Martin	L 201 960	42nd, 1943	New York, New York
Lucille Y. Mayo	L 200 238	28th, 1943	New York, New York
Alice M. McAlpine	L 115 192	34th, 1943	Springfield, Massachusetts
Carolyn A. Minkins	L 120 267	Unknown	Unknown
Gustine Moore	L 809 159	Unknown	Unknown
Ikalina M. Moore	L 604 921	Unknown	Unknown
Irmah L. Moore	L 600 260	11th, 1943	New York, New York
Marie W. Moore	L 803 376	Unknown	Unknown
Mary Alice Moore	L 303 578	11th, 1943	Magnolia, New Jersey
Virginia M. Moore	L 601 269	11th, 1943	Homer, Michigan

Name	Army Serial Number	Class and Year	Home
Mary Morgan	L 606 927	Unknown	Unknown
Rebecca C. Musgrove	L 803 410	Unknown	Unknown
Evelyn F. Overton	L 1 000 022	42nd, 1943	Washington, D.C.
Gladys E. Pace	L 1 000 610	44th, 1943	Washington, D.C.
Minnie P. Patterson	L 304 329	28th, 1943	Philadelphia, Pennsylvania
Calonia V. Powell	L 801 525	31st, 1943	Houston, Texas
Julia A. Rich	L 310 863	47th, 1953	Media, Pennsylvania
Lanora Robinson	L 215 385	Unknown	Unknown
Blanche L. Scott	L 303 576	11th, 1943	Washington, D.C.
Dorothy H. Scott	L 600 932	12th, 1943	Alton, Illinois
Evelyn C. Seace	Unknown	58th, 1945	Unknown
Martha A. Settle	L 1 000 091	35th, 1943	Norristown, Pennsylvania
Naomi Sikes	L 701 667	42nd, 1943	Lawton, Oklahoma
Juliette M. Simmons	L 402 537	11th, 1943	New Haven, Connecticut
Alma L. Sims	L 200 033	Unknown	Unknown
Alta E. Sims	Unknown	57th, 1945	Hampton, Virginia
Evelyn S. Smith	L 803 108	Unknown	Muskogee, Oklahoma
June E. Springs	L 604 508	Unknown	Unknown
Gussye D. Stewart	L 1 000 500	Unknown	Chicago, Illinois

Name	Army Serial Number	Class and Year	Home
Aubrey A. Stokes	L 1 000 267	51st, 1944	Gloucester, Virginia
Tenola Stoney	L 801 788	35th, 1943	Hempstead, Texas
Sophie G. Stranglin	L 402 049	11th, 1943	Atlanta, Georgia
Ella B. Tatum	L 800 726	36th, 1943	El Dorado, Arkansas
Camille Thomas	Unknown	30th, 1943	Unknown
Vashti B. Tonkins (Vashti T. Willis)	L 308 032	11th, 1943	Ashland, Virginia
La Mar Y. Turpin	Unknown	Unknown	Unknown
Corinne A. Walker	L 302 192	30th, 1943	Baltimore, Maryland
Lilla M. Walker	L 500 901	Unknown	Monterey, California
Katherine S. Watson	Unknown	Unknown	Unknown
Gladys C. Waynes	L 304 238	Unknown	Unknown
Zelda M. Webb	L 302 243	28th, 1943	Baltimore, Maryland
Jeanne C. Webster	L 303 950	29th, 1943	New York, New York
Charity E. White	L 802 972	35th, 1943	El Paso, Texas
Helma D. Williams	L 204 058	Unknown	Unknown
Julia M. Williams	L 402 781	29th, 1943	Birmingham, Alabama

Name	Army Serial Number	Class and Year	Home
Ernestine L. Woods (Ernestine W. White)	L 303 980	41st, 1943	Stamford, Connecticut

Sources: WAC School Study; scattered documents in RG 165 and RG 107; information from individuals in the corps; scattered special orders from Fort Des Moines records; official biographical records of officers of 6888th Central Postal Battalion; newspaper file at the Moorland-Spingarn Research Center; and SO 89 Headquarters United Kingdom Base, APO 413, par 27, March 30, 1945.

Appendix 5. Black Units in Field Assignments*

Army Posts

Location	Assignment	Commanding Officer**
Camp Beale, California	Clerical, motor transport, and other tasks at separation center	Marguerite L. Martin; later, Bernice G. Henderson
Fort Benning, Georgia	Various duties including clerical at reception center, post hospital, and postal section	Corrie S. Sherard; later, Harriette B. White
Fort Bragg, North Carolina	Ward attendants, technicians, and recreational therapists at regional hospital	Gertrude J. Peebles
Camp Breckenridge, Kentucky	Laundry workers and orderlies at post hospital and clerical duties at post headquarters	Myrtle E. Anderson
Camp Claiborne, Louisiana	Unknown	Unknown
Fort Clark, Texas	Clerical, motor transport, ward attendants, and orderlies	Unknown
Fort Custer, Michigan	Clerical and used in checking station at various tasks	Mildred L. Osby
Fort Dix, New Jersey	Mess attendants, ward attendants, orderlies, motor transport, and clerical	Ruth A. Lucas; later, Glendora Moore

*From available data. Some of these units or personnel therefrom served at two or more army installations.
**Some of these officers held two or more commands, and some of the units had two or more commanding officers during this period.

Location	Assignment	Commanding Officer
Camp Forrest, Tennessee	Ward attendants, orderlies, and technicians at station hospital	Abbie N. Campbell
Camp Gruber, Oklahoma	Unknown	Ina M. McFadden
Fort Huachuca, Arizona	Variety of technical, specialist, clerical, and mechanical jobs and technicians at post hospital	Frances C. Alexander, 32nd WAAC/WAC Co. Natalie F. Donalison, 33rd WAAC/WAC Co.
Fort Jackson, South Carolina	Ward attendants and technicians at regional hospital	Catherine G. Landry
Camp John T. Knight California	Clerical work in overseas supply division and attendants in the post hospital	Victoria J. Poole
Fort Knox, Kentucky	Cooks, mess attendants, waitresses, and ward attendants in post hospital, motor transport and clerical on post	Vera A. Harrison
Fort Leonard Wood, Missouri	Unknown	Unknown
Fort Lewis, Washington	Unknown	Irma J. Cayton
Camp Maxey, Texas	Ward orderlies, ward attendants, and technicians in post hospital, and clerical	Gladys Gould
Fort McClellan, Alabama	Worked in post hospital, postal section, service club, officers club, and as drivers	Corrie S. Sherard; later, Vashti B. Tonkins
Fort Oglethorpe, Georgia	Worked in post hospital	Abbie N. Campbell

Location	Assignment	Commanding Officer
Fort Ord, California	Unknown	Unknown
Fort Riley, Kansas	Ward attendants, nurses' aides, medical and laboratory technicians, and physiotherapy aides	Verneal M. Austin
Camp Rucker, Alabama	Unknown	Ethel E. Heywood
Fort Sam Houston, Texas	Truck jumpers, messengers, typists, and shipping clerks in shipping depot	Unknown
Camp Shanks, New York	Unknown	Oleta L. Crain
Fort Sheridan, Illinois	Worked on a variety of clerical jobs	Mildred L. Osby
Camp Sibert, Alabama	Unknown	Unknown
Staten Island Terminal, Stapleton, New York	Worked at the New York Port of Embarkation; medical, surgical, and dental technicians, attendants, and clerks	Margaret E. Barnes
Camp Stoneman, California	Unknown	Unknown
Camp Swift, Texas	Unknown	Unknown
Fort Wayne, Michigan	Unknown	Unknown
6888th Central Postal Directory, ETO	Operated the Central Postal Directory for the European Theater of Operation and directed mail to military personnel in the ETO	Charity E. Adams; later, Mary F. Kearney; later, Bernice G. Henderson

Army Air Force Bases

Location	Assignment	Commanding Officer
Amarillo Army Air Field, Texas	Unknown	Marie W. Moore
Douglas Army Air Field, Arizona	Aircraft maintenance, parachute packing, clerical, ward attendants, and laboratory technicians	Merceedees A. Jordan; later, Naomi A. Sikes
Fresno Air Service Command, California	Clerical, map reading, and editing	Unknown
Geiger Field, Washington	Variety of clerical duties in finance, supply, and administration, motor transport, and ward attendants and technicians in hospital	Verneal M. Austin; later, Ruth A. Lucas
Air Force Replacement Center, Kearns Field, Utah	Clerical duties on base, worked in base hospital, and as drivers	Annie L. Brown
Laurinburg-Maxton Army Air Base, North Carolina	Unknown	Unknown
Lemoore Army Air Field	Unknown	Oleta L. Crain
Lockbourne Army Air Base, Ohio	Unknown	Verneal M. Austin
Midland Army Air Base, Texas	Clerical duties on base and worked in base hospital	Ruth A. Lucas
Sioux City Army Air Base, Iowa	Worked in hospital, technical inspector's office, and post headquarters	Elizabeth C. Hampton; later, Helma D. Williams
Tuskegee Army Air Base, Alabama	Unknown	Unknown

Location	Assignment	Commanding Officer
Walla Walla Army Air Field, Washington	Clerks, typists, medical technicians, and airplane sheet metal workers	Blanche L. Scott; later, Ethel E. Heywood
Wendover Field, Utah	Medical technicians and clerks	Elizabeth C. Hampton

(According to the Army Air Force, blacks at the various bases worked in thirty-five different military occupation specialties, including as airplane electrical and instrument mechanics, automative equipment operators, medical administrative specialists, and photographic laboratory technicians [Memorandum from Headquarters, Army Air Force, to Jessie Pearl Rice, November 1, 1944, historical file RG 165].)

Army General Hospitals

Location	Assignment	Commanding Officer
Thomas E. England General Hospital, Atlantic City, New Jersey	Medical and surgical technicians, ward attendants, and medical aides	Ann G. Hall
Gardiner General Hospital, Chicago, Illinois	Medical and surgical technicians	Martha A. Settle
Halloran General Hospital, Staten Island, New York	Medical and surgical technicians, and ward attendants	Faracita Hall; later, Bernice G. Henderson
Percy Jones General Hospital, Fort Custer, Michigan	9951st TSU worked as mess attendants, ward attendants, medical and surgical aides, and clerks	Marguerite L. Martin
Lovell General Hospital, Fort Devens, Massachusetts	Orderlies	Tenola T. Stoney

Location	Assignment	Commanding Officer
Tilton General Hospital, Fort Dix, New Jersey	Mess attendants, ward attendants, medical aides, and drivers	Glendora Moore
Wakeman General Hospital, Camp Atterbury, Indiana	Medical and surgical technicians, laboratory aides, and ward attendants	Sarah E. Murphy; later, Jeanne G. Childs

Sources: Historical and decimal files RG 165; WAC School Study; newspaper file at Moorland-Spingarn Research Center; Army Directory at Center of Military History; Treadwell; and information from some women who served in these units.

Appendix 6. Number and Percentage of Blacks in the WAC, 1947–1978*

Month & Year	Total	Officers	Women	Number of Blacks			Percentage of Blacks		
				Total	Officers	Women	Total	Officers	Women
June 1950	7,259	708	6,551	648	19	629	8.9	2.6	9.6
June 1951	11,932	1,049	10,883	1,046	31	1,015	8.7	2.9	9.3
June 1952	11,456	1,228	10,228	1,332	41	1,291	11.6	3.2	12.6
June 1953	9,924	1,164	8,760	1,169	38	1,131	11.7	3.2	12.9
June 1954	7,803	1,016	6,787	869	31	838	11.1	3.0	12.3
June 1955	8,640	924	7,716	983	29	954	11.3	3.5	12.3
June 1956	8,661	891	7,770	1,061	32	1,029	11.8	3.5	13.2
June 1957	8,007	851	7,156	965	28	937	12.0	3.2	13.0
June 1958	7,853	779	7,074	933	24	909	11.8	3.0	12.8

June 1959	8,608	771	7,837	1,042	27	1,015	12.1	3.5	12.9
June 1960	9,053	774	8,279	1,183	28	1,155	13.0	3.6	13.9
June 1972	13,269	920	12,349	2,453	57	2,396	18.4	6.1	19.4
June 1973	17,551	1,094	16,457	3,188	60	3,128	18.1	5.4	19.0
June 1974	27,596	1,268	26,328	5,519	69	5,450	19.9	5.4	20.7
June 1975	39,171	1,468	37,703	8,122	91	8,031	20.7	6.1	21.3
Sept. 1976	46,413	1,952	44,461	9,785	104	9,681	21.0	5.3	21.7
Sept. 1977	48,548	2,454	46,094	11,537	244	11,293	23.7	9.9	24.4
Sept. 1978	52,996	2,704	50,292	14,688	276	14,412	27.7	10.2	28.6

*Data on blacks were not available from 1961 to 1971 and apparently were not maintained for these years. Data on officers include both commissioned and warrant officers. No blacks were warrant officers until 1950, and none from 1953 through 1960. There were five in 1972 and twelve in 1978. Source: "Strength of the Army" reports, copies of which may be found at the Center of Military History in Washington, D.C.

Appendix 7

HEADQUARTERS
FIRST WOMEN'S ARMY AUXILIARY CORPS
TRAINING CENTER
FORT DES MOINES, IOWA

CJC:sg
23 August 1943

MEMORANDUM:

TO   :   All concerned.

1. Effective on or about 1 September 1943, the Third Training Regiment (less Fourth Battalion and Twenty-eighth Company) will be converted from mixed white and colored to a colored regiment.

2. Effective on or about 1 September 1943, the First Training Regiment will be converted from O.C.S. and I.O.S. to a basic white training regiment.

3. The Third Training Regiment will be composed of the following units:

a. Regimental Headquarters

b. 1st Bn.-Cos. 6 through 13

c. 2nd Bn.-Cos. 14 through 21

4. The First Training Regiment will be composed of the following units:

a. Regimental Headquarters

b. 1st Bn.-Cos. 1 through 7

c. 2nd Bn.-Cos. 8 through 14

5. For the purpose of training of colored officers, the following officers will report to and understudy white officers now performing duties as indicated.

a. WAAC Regimental Comdr ---- 1st O Charity E. Adams

b. WAAC S-3 ------------------------ 1st O Dovey M. Johnson

c. WAAC S-4 ------------------------ 3rd O Corinne Walker

d. WAAC S-1 ------------------------ 3rd O Margaret Barnes

e. WAAC Bn CO, 1st Bn ---------- 1st O Sarah E. Emmert

f. WAAC Adj, 1st Bn -------------- 3rd O Martha Settle

g. WAAC Bn CO, 2nd Bn ---------- 1st O Ruth L. Freeman

h. WAAC Adj, 2nd Bn ------------- 3rd O Ikalina Moore

6. Upon transformation as indicated in Paragraph 1, units as indicated in Paragraph 3 will be staffed with full complement of officers and cadre in order that Government Property may be safeguarded and that company records be maintained.

7. The Colored WAAC Regimental Commander is responsible that suitably trained colored cadre is selected in sufficient time before transformation to insure that companies taken over from white officers are properly administered. In connection with this selection the WAAC Regimental Comdr will work with the TC Classification Officer.

8. The AUS Regimental Commander now functioning as such will maintain supervisory control as heretofore until directed otherwise.

9. For the purpose of administration, Company Twenty-eight, Third Regiment, will remain under command of CO Third Regiment. Personnel of Company Twenty-seven Third Regiment will be transferred about 1 Sept 43 to Company

Fourteen First Regiment, but will continue to occupy same barracks.

By order of Colonel McCOSKRIE:

C. J. CRUMM,
Capt., AGD,
Adjutant.

DISTRIBUTION

1 Each 1st and 3rd Regts
1 Each 4th Bn 3rd Regt
1 Each Officer Named in Par 5
1 Each Personnel
1 Each Classification
1 Director of Training
1 School Mess Officer
1 Billeting Officer
1 Post Engineer
1 Post Quartermaster
1 WAAC Supply
1 Surgeon

CHAPTER NOTES

Chapter 1

1. Chronological chart on the "History of the WAAC/WAC," Bethune Archives, Washington, D.C.
2. Recruiting brochures, posters, and literature on film clips and radio announcements and programs, Army G-1, WAAC/WAC Historical Background File Record Group 165, National Archives, Washington, D.C.; and SPWA 334.8, "Inaugural and Press Conference of Director," May 16, 1942, Army G-1, WAAC/WAC Decimal File Record Group 165, National Archives, Washington, D.C.
3. Mattie E. Treadwell, *Women's Army Corps* (Washington, D.C.: Government Printing Office, 1954), pp. 59, 590; and Philip McGuire, "Desegregation in the Armed Forces: Black Leadership, Protest and World War II," *Journal of Negro History* 68 (Spring 1983): 148. Periodically, the army adjutant general office sent to the commanding generals of the service commands notices specifying the recruitment needs of the corps. These notices usually included a reminder that "no more than 10%" should be black or gave precise comparable numbers for black and non-black recruits (see, for example, letter, Adjutant General Office to Commanding General, First Service Command, August 3, 1945, historical file RG 165).
4. Treadwell, pp. 59, 591.
5. Ibid., p. 59.
6. 201, Applicants for Office Candidate School, decimal file RG 165.
7. Papers in Bethune Archives.
8. John Hope Franklin, *From Slavery to Freedom: A History of Negro Americans,* 5th ed. (New York: Alfred A. Knopf, 1980), pp. 426–27.
9. Ibid., pp. 424–25; and McGuire, pp. 147, 151.
10. McGuire, pp. 148, 151; and *Chicago Defender,* November 2, 1942.

11. *Detroit Tribune,* August 29, 1942; and newspaper file on black women in the military, Moorland-Spingarn Research Center, Howard University, Washington, D.C.
12. Treadwell, p. 589; and interview with Dovey Johnson Round-tree, April 27, 1985.
13. Undated memorandum, historical file RG 165; and Lavinia L. Redd, "History of Military Training, WAAC/WAC Training" (unpublished manuscript, Center of Military History, Washington, D.C.), p. 10.
14. Undated memorandum on opening dates of the five centers, historical file RG 165; Redd, p. 10; Director Hobby to Truman K. Gibson, Jr., Acting Civilian Aide, Secretary of War, February 12, 1943, historical file RG 165; and SPWA 291.2, Director Hobby to Women's Editor of the *Afro-American,* August 18, 1943, decimal file RG 165. In Hobby's statement to Truman K. Gibson, nothing was mentioned about having black training complements at the other centers. The available records do not reveal the number of blacks trained at any of the training centers. However, the results of a survey of patron and memorial statements and one directory listing in five black WAAC/WAC souvenir reunion journals in which World War II service women's basic training centers were noted might throw some light on the matter. There were seventy-one instances where the location of the women's basic training was cited. In sixty-eight of these instances, the place was Fort Des Moines, and in the other three instances, the place was Fort Devens. None of the other training centers was cited. See First Negro WAAC/WAC Reunion Journal, October 13–16, 1978, Dallas, Texas; journal of Second Reunion of Black Military Women of WW II, October 16–19, 1980, Los Angeles, California; journal of Third WAC Reunion, August 19–22, 1982, Detroit, Michigan; journal of Fourth Black Women's Auxiliary Army Corps and Women's Army Corps Reunion, October 3–7, 1984, Atlanta, Georgia; and journal of Black WAAC/WAC and Women in the Service Reunion, October 2–5, 1986, Washington, D.C.
15. Redd, pp. 64–65, 70–90, 259–61; Army Directory: Continental U.S., June 1944, Center of Military History, Washington, D.C.; and SPMD-10, Memorandum to Surgeon General through Chief, Professional Administration Service, October 13, 1944, historical file RG 165.
16. For examples of reports, see WD WAC 353, History of Military Training WAAC/WAC Training, Army Service

Forces, March 1946, decimal file RG 165; and WD WAC 353, SPKTD 353, Training, WAC, Semimonthly Report, Commanding General, Seventh Service Command, Army Service Forces, to Director of WAC, July 1, 1944, and July 17, 1944, decimal file RG 165.

17. Ibid.; and Redd, pp. 200–218, 225, 226.

18. Mary A. Moore was assigned as executive officer of a company in Opportunity School (210.2 [29 Sept. 1943], A Training Command, F. U. McCoskrie to Commanding General, Headquarters WAC Training Command, October 2, 1943, decimal file RG 165). An official copy of the picture of the Special Training Unit company on parade is in the possession of the author. The February 27, 1943, issue of the *Chicago Defender* reported that Ann M. Clark was assigned as platoon commander of a non-black company at Fort Des Moines where she would serve as infantry drill instructor. The newspaper hailed this as the "first instance [of] a colored officer" being "assigned to an all-white company." The *Louisville* (Kentucky) *Defender* under the same dateline carried a similar report.

19. Report on Field Trip to Sixth and Seventh Service Commands by Harriet M. West, May 17, 1943, historical file RG 165; SPWA 320.5 (5-15-43), T. B. Catron, Colonel, Military Advisor and Executive, to Office of Chief of Staff, War Manpower Board, May 28, 1943, decimal file RG 165; Redd, p. 10; Treadwell, pp. 591–92; and newspaper file at Moorland-Spingarn Research Center.

20. Report on Trip to Fort Des Moines, n.d. (inspection tour began November 2, 1942), historical file RG 165. The problem of a desegregated mess hall had been discussed at the War Department prior to the dispatch of a staff officer to Fort Des Moines. In October, an individual in the office of the assistant secretary of war, who described himself as "being a damn Yank," suggested non-segregated messes at Fort Des Moines. He noted, "I still cannot see that it would do a white at a military post any permanent harm to eat food in proximity with a colored person." The staff officer who made the inspection in November 1942 recommended in his report that on Saturdays and Sundays blacks and non-blacks "be permitted to sit where they like in the mess hall." He felt that "those who desire to eat with their race will do so," and "those who would like an opportunity to become better acquainted with the opposite race will have a chance." See General Correspondence of John J. McCloy, Office of the Secretary of War, Assistant Secretary

of War, 021-031.1, memorandum from J. M. H. to John J.
McCloy, October 7, 1942, RG 107; and Report on Trip to Fort
Des Moines, n.d. (November 1942), historical file RG 165.

21. *Philadelphia Tribune,* October 12, 1942, and January 9, 1943;
210.2 (29 Sept. 1943), A Training Command, F. U. McCoskrie
to Commanding General, Headquarters, WAC Training Command, October 2, 1943, decimal file RG 165; copy of résumé
of Charity Edna Adams Earley on file at the Center of Military
History; and *Des Moines Register,* September 22, 1943.

22. 201, Applicants for Officer Candidate School, decimal file RG
165; and undated notes of interview with Vera G. Campbell.

23. Undated notes of interview with Vera G. Campbell.

24. Undated notes of interview with Ina McRae.

25. A copy of this memorandum from the Fort Des Moines records
is in the possession of the author. The September 4, 1943,
issue of the *Chicago Defender* published the name of one of the
designated battalion commanders, who was a native of Chicago.

26. Interview with Dovey Johnson Roundtree, April 27, 1985; and
notes from a journal maintained during her period of service by
Lieutenant Martha Settle. In reference to the argument about
promotions of black officers on the post, except for those who
were commissioned with the first Officer Candidate School
class, none had been promoted at this point. Some 568 officers
were promoted on December 23, 1942, 81 of them to the rank
of first officer, the equivalent of captain. These promotions
included 35 blacks, 4 of them to first officer rank. The 4 were
Charity E. Adams, Frances C. Alexander, Natalie F. Donaldson, and Harriet M. West. At that time, only Adams was
stationed at Fort Des Moines; Alexander and Donaldson were
company commanders at Fort Huachuca, Arizona; and West
was assigned to the Pentagon. Later, on August 23, 1943, West
was among a group of women elevated to the rank of field
director, the equivalent of major. On September 18, 1943,
some ten days after the revocation of the reorganization plan,
Adams was promoted to major (press release, January 4, 1943,
historical file RG 165; *New York Age,* January 9, 1943;
Significant Events in the Progress of the WAAC/WAC, 1943–
1944, n.d., historical file RG 165; and *Des Moines Register,*
September 22, 1943).

27. Interview with Dovey Johnson, April 27, 1985; and notes from
the journal of Lieutenant Settle. Reference is made to this
episode in Treadwell, p. 597.

28. Ibid.
29. 291.2, Detroit Office of the NAACP to Mr. Leslie Perry, Director of the Washington, D.C., Office, September 29, 1943, decimal file RG 165; 291.2, National Council of Negro Women to Director Hobby, n.d., historical file RG 165; and interview with Dovey Johnson Roundtree, April 27, 1985.
30. A copy of the memorandum is in the possession of the author.
31. On the transfer of black soldiers from Fort Des Moines to Fort Dodge, see undated memorandum, historical file RG 165. Interview with Dovey Johnson Roundtree on October 31, 1987, and Ethel Heywood Smith on May 25, 1988, provided information on black enlisted men visiting the service club.
32. Memorandum from Catherine L. Settle to author, December 28, 1983.
33. Ibid.; *Des Moines Register,* September 12, 1943; and interview with Ethel Heywood Smith, May 25, 1988.
34. Interview with Ethel Heywood Smith, May 25, 1988; undated notes of interview with Vera G. Campbell; and scattered special orders from Fort Des Moines records of attached unassigned status of some black officers. At times more than thirty black officers were stationed at Fort Des Moines. Some were attached unassigned, and others had returned from tours of duty at service schools or for changes of assignments. See, for example, 210.3 (25 Sept. 1943) O-P, Director Hobby to Director of Military Personnel, Army Service Forces, October 7, 1943, decimal file RG 165, which indicates that thirty-nine black officers were stationed at Fort Des Moines at that time.
35. Papers in Bethune Archives; and interview with Dovey Johnson Roundtree, May 4, 1985. On Army Regulation 210-10 of December 20, 1940, which dealt with officers clubs on federal property and a directive issued on March 10, 1943, which required the removal of signs designating facilities for blacks and whites, see Morris J. MacGregor, Jr., *Integration of the Armed Forces, 1940–1965* (Washington, D.C.: Government Printing Office, 1981), p. 45.
36. Interview with Dovey Johnson Roundtree, May 4, 1985; and letter from a Negro WAC to Walter White, April 4, 1945, NAACP Papers, Manuscript Division, Library of Congress, Washington, D.C.
37. General Court-Martial Orders No. 158, Fort Des Moines, January 8–10, 1945.
38. United States v. Futrell et al., CM 274866, United States Army Judiciary, Department of the Army, Washington, D.C.

39. Ibid.; and *A Manual for Courts-Martial, U.S. Army* (Washington, D.C.: Government Printing Office, 1928), corrected to April 20, 1943, p. 225.
40. United States v. Futrell et al.
41. Ibid.
42. Ibid.; and AGPO-S-201, Pace, Gladys E., Adjutant General Office, War Department, December 13, 1945.
43. SPWA 320.2, T. B. Catron to Director Hobby, June 3, 1943, decimal file RG 165.
44. Ibid.
45. SPWA 335.11, Documents on Association Between Women's Army Corps Officers and Enlisted Men and Male Officers and Enlisted Women, December 23, 1943; January 6, 1944; January 8, 1944; and January 12, 1944, decimal file RG 165.
46. 250.3–291, Captain Lee to Colonel Hobby, April 11, 1944, decimal file RG 165; and WDGAP 201, Assistant Chief of Staff, G-1, to Judge Advocate General, March 15, 1945, decimal file RG 165.
47. 341.7, For Anyone Writing History, memorandum of Colonel Boyce, November 27, 1945, decimal file RG 165. The practice of local control continued to cause problems under Boyce.
48. Redd, p. 10; WD 353, Memorandum to the Director, October 3, 1944, decimal file RG 165; and WD 353, Consolidation of training centers, December 22, 1944. The National Civilian Advisory Committee was selected by the War Department to give the department counsel on the WAAC/WAC. It was composed of twenty-three prominent women from all sections of the country and various fields of endeavor and met at stated intervals. Bethune was the only black on this committee. For some of the activities of this committee, see the papers in the Bethune Archives.
49. *Afro-American* (Washington), March 10, 1945.

Chapter 2

1. Treadwell, p. 589; Folder on enrollment of Japanese-American women in the WAAC in historical file RG 165; 330.14, Folder on rumors and stories on WAAC/WAC morality, decimal file RG 165; WD Report No. B 80, What the Soldier Thinks of the WAC, Research Branch, Morale Service Division, Army Service Forces, December 10, 1943, decimal file RG 165; and 330.14, Letters and articles in the *Washington Post*, June 30,

1943, decimal file RG 165. The historical and decimal files contain several folders of reports and documents on rumors, innuendos, and attitudes that affected morale and recruiting. So concerned were the corps and the army about this matter that they commissioned the research department of Young and Rubican, Inc., under the direction of George Gallup to do an in-depth study on the problem. This firm produced a multi-volume report entitled *National Study of Public Opinion Toward the Women's Army Corps* and prepared a scrapbook of "Unfavorable WAC Newspaper Publicity" in 1944. The report suggested ways to deal with the problem. A number of recruiting conferences and seminars were held to devise strategies to overcome the problem and to increase the number of recruits. See, for example, SPWA 000.7, decimal file RG 165; WDLSP 337, Report on Conference in Chicago, Illinois, February 21–23, 1944, decimal file RG 165; SPWA 341, Civilian Committees for WAC Recruiting, January 31, 1943, decimal file RG 165; WA 341, Recruiting Conference, May 7–8, 1943, decimal file RG 165; and WDGAP 341, Comment on public opinion concerning the WAC and factors affecting it, March 21, 1944, RG 165.

2. Report, statistical history of the WAAC/WAC, June 1943, historical file RG 165; and Memorandum, May 29, 1943, historical file RG 165. The age requirements for enrolling in the corps varied according to the needs of the service. At the beginning, the age requirements were 20 to 49 inclusive. In February 1943, a brochure listed the age limits as 21 to 44 inclusive. In late 1944, in order to obtain women for hospital companies, the age for entry was set at 20 to 49 again. See memorandum on qualifications for enrolling, August 29, 1942, historical file RG 165; memorandum on age requirements, December 30, 1942, historical file RG 165; "Life in the WAAC," issued February 15, 1943, a copy in historical file RG 165; Office of War Information, Domestic Radio Bureau, Army Hospitals Need WACs, n.d. (1944), historical file RG 165; and AGSPR-1 341 WAC, recruiting for army general hospitals, historical file RG 165.

3. SPWA 334.8, conference, May 16, 1942, decimal file RG 165.

4. WA 080, Esther V. Cooper, Executive Secretary, Southern Negro Youth Congress to Colonel Hobby, June 8, 1942, decimal file RG 165; and 291.2, report of the National Council of Negro Women, n.d., decimal file.

5. Treadwell, pp. 591, 592; and papers in Bethune Archives.

6. Ulysses Lee, *The Employment of Negro Troops* (Washington, D.C.: Government Printing Office, 1966), p. 423; Treadwell, pp. 59, 592; and interview with Dovey Johnson Roundtree, November 7, 1987.

7. Treadwell, p. 592.

8. Memorandum on assignment of black officers to recruiting duties, n.d., historical file RG 165; Office of the Director to John W. Davis, president of West Virginia State College, January 15, 1943, historical file RG 165; newspaper file, Moorland-Spingarn Research Center; and papers in the Bethune Archives.

9. SPWA 341, Dovey M. Johnson and Ruth A. Lucas to Harriet M. West, Office of Inspection and Control, Headquarters WAAC, November 22, 1942, decimal file RG 165.

10. Ibid. The NAACP regarded the paucity of pictures of black WACs in the press, newsreels, and brochures as a handicap in the recruiting of blacks (Walter White to Natalie Donaldson, November 25, 1942, NAACP Papers).

11. SPWA 341, Dovey M. Johnson and Ruth A. Lucas to Harriet M. West, Office of Inspection and Control, Headquarters WAAC, December 22, 1942, decimal file RG 165.

12. Newspaper clippings and accounts, many undated, of Johnson's recruiting activities are in Bethune Archives; and SPWA 291.2, L. Virgil Williams, Executive Secretary of Dallas Negro Chamber of Commerce, to Director Hobby, July 2, 1943, decimal file RG 165.

13. SPWA 341, Harriette (B. White) to Harriet M. West (November 1942), decimal file RG 165.

14. Sgt. Maj. Grendel Howard, "Carrying Forth a Tradition," *Soldiers*, February 1985, p. 29. For recruiting activities of some of the other black officers, see the *Washington Star*, November 19, 1942; *Norfolk Journal and Guide*, November 21, 1942, and March 6, 1943; and *Philadelphia Tribune*, October 19, 1942, and November 7, 1942.

15. *Richmond Afro-American*, February 13, 1943; *Portsmouth Star*, April 11, 1943; and Album and Scrapbook of Blanche L. Scott, Alexandria, Virginia.

16. Newspaper file on black women in the military, Moorland-Spingarn Research Center; and interview with Dovey Johnson Roundtree, November 7, 1987. On the recruiting activities of Ethel E. Heywood and some of those of Ina M. McFadden and Evelyn F. Greene, see Heywood's Album and Scrapbook at the Bethune Archives and letter from Heywood to District Re-

cruiting and Induction Office, Syracuse, New York, March 8, 1943, in Bethune Archives.

17. Treadwell, p. 593.
18. Memorandum, George F. Martin to Director of WAAC, May 24, 1943, historical file RG 165; SPWA 291.2, L. Virgil Williams, Executive Secretary of Dallas Negro Chamber of Commerce to Director Hobby, July 2, 1943, decimal file RG 165; papers in Bethune Archives; newspaper file, Moorland-Spingarn Research Center; and Harold A. Edlund to Colonel T. B. Catron, Military Advisor and Executive, Headquarters WAAC, July 14, 1943, historical file RG 165.
19. SPWA 291.2, Elizabeth C. Strayhorn, Acting Director, to L. Virgil Williams, Executive Secretary of Dallas Negro Chamber of Commerce, July 17, 1943, decimal file RG 165. A similar communication was sent to Walter White, Executive Secretary of the NAACP, under the same file number. Documents in the Bethune Archives show that at least four black recruiting officers received reassignment orders dated June 8, 1943.
20. Treadwell, p. 594; and SPWA 330.14, James B. McGhee to Colonel Hobby, May 8, 1943, decimal file RG 165. For another instance of complaints of this nature, see SPWA 330.14, John C. Leissler to Congressman H. W. Summers, January 14, 1943, decimal file RG 165.
21. Newspaper clippings and articles of Johnson's activities in Ohio are in the Bethune Archives.
22. SPWA 080, Edwina T. Glascor, Assistant Director of Youth Department, Columbus Urban League, to General Don C. Faith, Director Field Survey Branch WAC, December 20, 1943, decimal file RG 165; same to same, December 29, 1943, decimal file RG 165; SPWA 080, Patricia M. Lee, First Lieutenant WAC, to Edwina T. Glascor, January 12, 1944, decimal file RG 165; SPWA 080, Edwina T. Glascor to Director Hobby, February 7, 1944, decimal file RG 165; and SPWA 080, Director Hobby to Edwina T. Glascor, February 12, 1944, decimal file RG 165. The theme of the recruiting seminars and conferences was "go out and get more WACs." See, for example, WA 341, Recruiting Conference held in Omaha, Nebraska, March 3, 1944, decimal file RG 165, and reports of conferences cited in note 1 of chapter 2, above.
23. Letter from Balm L. Leavell, Jr., secretary-treasurer of Negro Labor Relations League of Chicago, to Walter White, April 12, 1945, NAACP Papers
24. Interview with Dovey Johnson Roundtree, April 27, 1985. See

also Howard, p. 29; WDWAC 341, memorandum from Director Hobby to Chief of Staff, March 21, 1944, decimal file RG 165 on soldier publications; and SPWA 341, memorandum Army Service Forces, Headquarters, Sixth Service Command to Ward Department, decimal file RG 165 report, and comments on questionnaires selected from 53 percent of the enlisted men at Camp Ellis, Illinois, whose attitude toward WAACs was unfavorable, and was regarded as "too important to overlook."

25. SPWA 330.14, Rosalie de Jesus to Congresswoman Edith N. Rogers, December 14, 1943, decimal file RG 165. In this letter, the enlisted woman complained that (among other things) the soldiers broke into the barracks, were arrested, and were placed in the stockade, but, she stated, her commanding officer refused to press charges against them.

26. Bulletin, Army Hospitals Need WACs, Officer of War Information, Domestic Radio Bureau, n.d., historical file RG 165; AGPR-1 341 WAC, Recruiting for Army General Hospitals, January 1945, historical file RG 165; and newspaper file, Moorland-Spingarn Research Center. The National Civilian Advisory Committee was told at its meeting at Fort Des Moines, February 16–18, 1945, that it was assumed that black applicants would be willing to volunteer for service at the general hospitals (memorandum accompanying report of this meeting, n.d., historical file RG 165).

27. Treadwell, p. 590; Lee, p. 423; and Adjutant General to Commanding General, First Service Command, August 3, 1945, historical file RG 165. Other periodic notes to the commanding generals of the service commands can be found scattered throughout the historical file.

28. Memorandum accompanying report of meeting of National Civilian Advisory Committee at Fort Des Moines, February 16–18, 1945, historical file RG 165; SPWA 702, WAC medical rejection rate, Harold F. Dorn to Director Hobby, September 15, 1945, decimal file RG 165; Information pertaining to Women's Army Corps, January 1–April 30, 1944; May 10, 1944; historical file RG 165; Memorandum on enlistments in the corps from April 1–7, 1945, n.d., historical file RG 165; "Summary of Information on Negro Women Who Have Served or Are Serving in the Women's Army Corps, 1942–1963," unpublished study prepared by the Division of Doctrine and Literature, United States Women's Army Corps School, Fort McClellan, Alabama, October 1963 (hereafter

referred to as WAC School Study); and newspaper file, Moorland-Spingarn Research Center.

29. Memorandum from G. T. Gifford, Lieutenant Colonel, Infantry, Director of Personnel, WAAC, to Adjutant General, November 23, 1942, historical file RG 165; Memorandum on data on black enrollment, April 30, 1943, historical file RG 165; and SPWA 341, Harriette (B. White) to Harriet M. West, n.d. (November 1942), decimal file RG 165.

30. Different figures are given for the size of the first OCS class. Treadwell, on p. 590, shows a class size of 440, including 40 blacks. Redd, on pp. 259 and 270, indicates that 444, including 41 blacks, entered the first OCS class. The black newspaper accounts show that 40 blacks were in the first class (see newspaper file, Moorland-Spingarn Research Center). Redd, who reportedly used the papers and documents from Fort Des Moines, probably has the correct figures of those selected for the first class.

31. Treadwell, p. 765, 777; "Strength of the Army" reports, Center of Military History, Washington, D.C.; and Report on significant events in the progress of the WAAC/WAC, 1943–1944, n.d., historical file RG 165. The failure of 343 officers and 14,607 enlisted women to reenlist when the WAAC converted to the WAC represented a loss of about one-fourth of the strength of the corps (Report on significant events in the progress of the WAAC/WAC, 1943–1944). It was not until 1948 that the Women's Army Corps became an integral part of the Regular Army. The Women's Armed Services Integration Act, which became law on June 12, 1948, made the corps a component of the Regular Army and the Army Reserve.

32. These numbers and percentages do not include the warrant officers.

33. A number of black newspapers carried the names and hometowns of the thirty-six black graduates of the first OCS class, including the *Philadelphia Tribune* in its September 5, 1942, issue. The Bethune Archives also has a list of the names.

34. Press release, January 9, 1943, historical file RG 165. The nine who were commissioned were Ethel E. Heywood, Irmah L. Moore, Mary A. Moore, Virginia M. Moore, Sophie Gay Stranglin, Blanche L. Scott, Juliette M. Simmons, Vashti B. Tonkins, and Virginia Marshall Cheeks. The last person's name and army serial number are noted in the WAC School Study, and she is cited as having been a graduate of the eleventh class.

See also Special Orders No. 268, Headquarters, Third Women's Army Corps Training Center, Fort Oglethorpe, Georgia, October 16, 1943, par. 1, for list of forty-second class, and par. 3 for the transfer of its four black members to Fort Des Moines for assignment and duty. Bertie M. Edwards, a member of this class, identified the blacks in the class. SPWA 210.2, Memorandum, Lieutenant Colonel Brown to Anne E. Alinder, February 26, 1944, decimal file RG 165, lists the entering dates and dates of commissioning of OCS classes. Copy of Special Orders No. 268 is in possession of author.

35. Memorandum, Director Hobby to Truman K. Gibson, Jr., Acting Civilian Aide to Secretary of War, February 12, 1943, historical file RG 165; Confidential Memorandum, Lieutenant Parker to Director Hobby, April 13, 1943, historical file RG 165; and SPWA 291.2, Gretchen M. Thorp, Technical Information Division, to Florence Murray, August 7, 1943, decimal file RG 165.

36. Memorandum accompanying report of the meeting of the National Civilian Advisory Committee at Fort Des Moines, February 16–18, 1945, historical file RG 165.

Chapter 3

1. SPWA 334.8, Inaugural and Press Conference of the Director, May 16, 1942, decimal file RG 165; WA 291.21, William F. Pearson, Colonel, Adjutant General's Office, Headquarters, May 27, 1942, decimal file RG 165; and Treadwell, p. 590.

2. Walter White, the NAACP secretary, sent telegrams or letters to Congresswoman Edith N. Rogers and Congressmen John W. McCormack, Joseph W. Martin, Everett Dirksen, and others seeking their support for a non-discrimination clause. All of these communications were dated February 2, 1942, and may be found among the NAACP Papers in the Manuscript Division of the Library of Congress.

3. Papers in Bethune Archives.

4. Ibid.

5. Copy of Jeanetta Welch Brown's letter to Colonel Hobby dated July 26, 1944, is in Bethune Archives; and Horace R. Cayton to Armed Forces Induction Station, Chicago, Illinois, July 8, 1944, Office of Assistant Secretary of War, Civilian Aide to the Secretary of War, subject file RG 107.

6. *Chicago Defender,* September 5, 1942; SPWA 291.2, Memo-

randum for War Department, Bureau of Public Relations, Report on Charles P. Howard on Negro Officer Candidates at WAAC Training Center, J. Noel Macy to Lieutenant Colonel Can, Assistant Director, September 12, 1942, decimal file RG 165; and Interview with Dovey J. Roundtree, October 31, 1987.

7. Interview with Dovey J. Roundtree, October 31, 1987.
8. Ibid.
9. Ibid.; and SPWA 291.21, letter from Walter White, Executive Secretary of NAACP, jointly addressed to Henry L. Stimson, Secretary of War, and Mrs. Oveta Culp Hobby, Director of the WAAC, October 28, 1942, decimal file RG 165.
10. *Chicago Defender,* September 5, 1942; and newspaper file, Moorland-Spingarn Research Center.
11. Memorandum in Bethune Archives; *Birmingham World,* July 24, 1942; and WD WAAC 291.2, Report of National Council of Negro Women, n.d., decimal file RG 165.
12. *Birmingham World,* July 24, 1942. The National Council of Negro Women, of which Bethune was a charter member, in its undated report to the War Department, explicitly stated that it was "working towards the goal of full integration" in the corps. The council wanted black officers trained for recruiting duties, sent to all specialized schools offered to non-black officers, assigned to operational jobs in the field and at headquarters at the Pentagon, and used as counselors at Fort Des Moines and at other posts where black enlisted women were stationed. The council's report further sought to have black enlisted women assigned to the Adjutant General's Office at headquarters (WD WAAC 291.2, Report of the National Council of Negro Women, n.d., decimal file RG 165).
13. WD 291.21, P. L. Prattis, Executive Editor, *Pittsburgh Courier,* to Director Hobby, August 11, 1942, decimal file RG 165.
14. WD SPWA 333.9, Don C. Faith, Colonel, Infantry, Commanding Officer of Fort Des Moines, to Director of WAAC, August 24, 1942, decimal file RG 165.
15. Treadwell, p. 592; and WAC School Study.
16. SPWA 291.21, Walter White jointly addressed to Henry L. Stimson and Mrs. Oveta Culp Hobby, October 28, 1942, decimal file RG 165.
17. Report on trip to Fort Des Moines, n.d. (visitation began November 2, 1942), historical file RG 165; Redd, pp. 259–60, 270–71; WAC School Study; and Interviews with Blanche L. Scott on April 4, 1988, and Juliette M. Simmons and Ethel

Heywood Smith on May 22, 1988, three members of the eleventh OCS class. See also Appendix 3. Only in the army air force were officer training programs segregated (Franklin, p. 430).

18. Report on a trip to Fort Des Moines, n.d. (visitation began November 2, 1942), historical file RG 165; and *Afro-American* (Baltimore), November 21, 1942.

19. Letter from Walter White to Natalie Donaldson, November 25, 1942, NAACP Papers, Manuscript Division, Library of Congress, Washington, D.C.

20. Redd, pp. 260 and 270; and interviews with Blanche L. Scott on April 4, 1988, Juliette Simmons on May 22, 1988, and Ethel Heywood Smith on May 22, 1988, and June 6, 1988; Scott, Simmons, and Smith were three members of the eleventh OCS class. See also Appendix 3.

21. Papers in Bethune Archives; and Walter White, Executive Secretary of the NAACP, to William Hastie, Civilian Aide to the Secretary of War, October 28, 1942, subject file RG 107.

22. Ibid.

23. Report on trip to Fort Des Moines, n.d. (visitation began November 2, 1942), historical file RG 165. Some of the other recommendations made by this staff officer were discussed in Chapter 1.

24. Letter, Thelma B. Brown to Bethune, papers in Bethune Archives; WAC School Study; Third Black WAC Reunion Souvenir Journal; Fourth WAAC/WAC Reunion Souvenir Journal; and WD WAC 353, SPKTD 353, Report to Conference of WAC Staff Directors and Senior Officers, July 11–12, 1944, historical file RG 165.

25. AGOT-R 332 Band (July 28, 1944), a folder of correspondence on the band with requests for information, protests, and replies, Office of Assistant Secretary of War, Civilian Aide to the Secretary of War, subject file RG 107; and Letter, Lieutenant Thelma B. Brown to Bethune, Bethune Archives.

26. Copy of letter from Walter White to Henry L. Stimson, July 18, 1944, in Bethune Archives. See also AGOT-R 332 Band (July 28, 1944) correspondence on band, Office of Assistant Secretary of War, Civilian Aide to the Secretary of War, subject file RG 107. Lieutenant Thelma B. Brown in her letter to Bethune sounded the alarm on the plight of the band (letter in Bethune Archives).

27. Copies of and responses to these letters and others may be found in WD WAC 330.14 folder on band, decimal file RG

165; or AGOT-R 332 Band (July 28, 1944) folder, Civilian Aide to the Secretary of War, subject file RG 107. Some of these letters were addressed to Director Hobby, some to Secretary Stimson, some to Eleanor Roosevelt, and others to Franklin D. Roosevelt. Stimson was a firm believer in segregation. He criticized the "foolish leaders of the colored race" who, he said, wanted "at bottom social equality," which he felt would never happen "because of the impossibility of race mixture by marriage." At the same time, Stimson complained about Eleanor Roosevelt's "intrusive and impulsive folly," which he regarded as the cause of the criticism of the army's racial policy (MacGregor, *Integration,* p. 21, quoting from Stimson's diary).

28. Papers in Bethune Archives; and AGOT-R 332 Band (July 28, 1944) folder, subject file RG 107.

29. Papers in Bethune Archives; and WD WAC 330.14, folder on band, decimal file RG 165.

30. 021-031.1, letter from Dallas G. Corbin, President of Vallejo Branch of the NAACP, to Franklin D. Roosevelt, President of the United States, August 2, 1944; and 020-031.1, memorandum from John J. McCloy to Deputy Chief of Staff, August 7, 1944, Office of the Secretary of War, Assistant Secretary of War, General Correspondence of John J. McCloy, RG 107.

31. AGOT-R 332 Band (July 28, 1944) folder, subject file RG 107; and WD WAC 330.14 folder on band, decimal file RG 165; papers in Bethune Archives; and WAC School Study.

32. WD WAC 330.14, Lieutenant Colonel Jessie Pearl Rice to Bethune, August 14, 1944, decimal file RG 165. Similar letters were sent to other black leaders and organizations.

33. WD WAC 330.14, Colonel Hobby to Ike Small, Chairman, Racial Justice Committee of the Des Moines Interracial Commission, November 23, 1944, decimal file RG 165; and WAC School Study.

34. Treadwell, p. 59; WA 291.2, memorandum from Harold P. Tasker, Lieutenant Colonel, GSC, Executive Officer to Director of WAAC, August 15, 1942, decimal file RG 165; and memorandum from Colonel Don Faith, Commandant, First WAAC Training Center, to Director of WAAC, on results of conferences of August 29–31, 1942, decimal file RG 165.

35. SPWA 291.21, Harold P. Tasker, Lieutenant Colonel, Director of Operations, WAAC, to Commanding General, First Fighter Command through Commanding General Second Service Command, October 2, 1942, decimal file RG 165;

SPWA 346, Harold P. Tasker, Lieutenant Colonel, Director of Operations, WAAC, to Commandant at Fort Des Moines, December 16, 1942, decimal file RG 165; and SPWA 320.2, Howard Clark, Lieutenant Colonel, Headquarters, WAAC, to WAAC Service Commands Directors in First, Second, Third, and Fourth Service Commands, February 15, 1943, decimal file RG 165. Both the corps and the army had information that the Aircraft Warning Service had denied black civilians employment. The mayor of New York City, on behalf of one of his constituents who had been unable to obtain a job, sought information from the War Department on policy for hiring in the Aircraft Warning Service. The mayor was subsequently informed by the Labor Department that his constituent was rejected for employment because she was black (SPWA 291.2, Mayor of New York to War Department, July 21, 1942, decimal file RG 165; and SPWA 291.2, Secretary of Labor to Mayor of New York, and Mayor of New York to Lawrence W. Cramer of FEPO, July 30, 1942, decimal file RG 165).

36. *Afro-American* (Washington), July 10, 1943.
37. Ibid.; and newspaper file at Moorland-Spingarn Research Center.
38. *P.M.*, March 21, 1945; and newspaper file at Moorland-Spingarn Research Center.
39. *Washington Post*, March 23, 1945; *Pittsburgh Courier*, April 28, 1945; and newspaper file at Moorland-Spingarn Research Center.
40. Ibid.
41. Ibid.; 291.2, folder on "1945 Lovell General Hospital," decimal file RG 165; 291.2, copy of letter from Charles H. Houston to Bethune, April 26, 1945, decimal file RG 165; and 021-031.1, General Correspondence of John J. McCloy, Assistant Secretary of War, documents and letters addressed to him and from him on the case, March–April, 1945, RG 107.
42. *Washington Post*, March 23, 1945; newspaper file at Moorland-Spingarn Research Center; and 291.2, copy of letter from Charles H. Houston to Bethune, April 26, 1945, decimal file RG 165.
43. Newspaper file at Moorland-Spingarn Research Center.
44. Ibid. Some protests, especially on the sentence, came from non-black civilians. See WD WAC 330.14 decimal file RG 165, on Lovell General Hospital.
45. Newspaper file at Moorland-Spingarn Research Center. Other accounts of this case may be found in the *Washington Post*,

March 21, 1945, and April 28, 1945; *Norfolk Journal and Guide,* April 21, 1945; *P.M.,* March 21, 1945; and *Pittsburgh Courier,* April 28, 1945.

46. Report of Action, March 16–19, 1945: Daily Reports, historical file RG 165; and WD WAC 330.14, William T. Granaham to Secretary of War Henry L. Stimson, March 13, 1945, decimal file RG 165. Other letters of inquiry and concern about this case may be found in WD WAC 330.14, decimal file RG 165. The army ran down the name of the black enlisted woman who had written to Congressman Granaham; Major General Sherman Miles was very interested in knowing who among the women were writing to congressmen about the incident (SPBVW 220.3, letter from Sherman Miles, Commanding General, First Service Command, to Headquarters, March 26, 1945, decimal file RG 165).

47. 291.2, Charles H. Houston to Bethune, April 26, 1945, decimal file RG 165; and 200-300.5, Louis R. Lautier, Administrative Office of the Civilian Aide to the Secretary of War, to Carl Murphy, President of the *Afro-American* newspaper, April 26, 1945, decimal file RG 165. In response to a letter from Congressman Emanuel Celler of New York, Major General Sherman Miles stated that the black unit's commanding officer had ordered the women to return to work (021-031.1, letter from Sherman Miles to Emanuel Celler, House of Representatives, March 24, 1945, Office of the Secretary of War, Assistant Secretary of War, General Correspondence of John J. McCloy, RG 107).

48. WD WAC 291.2, Inspector General's Report on Colored WACs Stationed at Fort Devens, Massachusetts, excerpts from confidential report, n.d., decimal file RG 165; SPWA 291.2, Memorandum, August 6, 1945, decimal file RG 165; and WD WAC 291.2, Colonel Hobby to Women's Editor, *Afro-American* newspaper, August 18, 1945, decimal file RG 165.

49. Letter from a Negro WAC to Roy Wilkins, acting secretary of the NAACP, April 4, 1945, NAACP Papers.

50. Ibid. Apparently no black staff field worker was assigned. Scattered throughout the NAACP Papers are several letters from black WACs calling attention to problem areas in the corps or thanking the organization for helping to resolve specific problems.

51. *Amsterdam-Star News* (New York), July 28, 1945; and *New York Age,* August 18, 1945.

52. Ibid.; and SPVID, Memorandum, Headquarters, Fifth Service

Command, Fort Hayes, Columbus, Ohio, July 27, 1945, historical file RG 165.

53. Ibid.
54. Ibid.; and 021-031.1, Letter from John J. McCloy to Gaten Little, Chicago Civil Liberties Committee, July 23, 1945, General Correspondence of John J. McCloy, RG 107.
55. *New York Age,* August 18, 1945.
56. 021-031.1, Letter from Harrison A. Gerharde to William Warley, Editor of the *Louisville News,* October 11, 1945, General Correspondence of John J. McCloy, RG 107; 021-031.1 (ASW 021 WAC), Letter from Charles W. McCarthy, General Staff Corps, to Assistant Secretary of War, October 20, 1945, General Correspondence of John J. McCloy, RG 107.
57. Morris J. MacGregor and Bernard C. Nalty, eds., *Blacks in the United States Armed Forces: Basic Documents* (Wilmington: Scholarly Resources, 1977), 5: 288–90.
58. Ibid.
59. Ibid.
60. SPHW, Report of Third Service Command WAC Civilian Advisory Committee to WAC Section, February 10, 1945. A copy of this report may be found in the Bethune Archives.
61. Letter from "A Very Unhappy, Disillusioned WAC Officer" to Truman K. Gibson, Jr., n.d., Office of Assistant Secretary of War, Civilian Aide to the Secretary, subject file RG 107; Letter from Constance E. Nelson to the *Houston Informer,* May 26, 1944, a copy in subject file RG 107, Office of Assistant Secretary of War, Civilian Aide to Secretary of War; and *Afro-American* (Washington), March 3, 1945.
62. *Afro-American* (Washington), March 3, 1945.

Chapter 4

1. AGO 320.2 WAAC, Adjutant General's Office to All Service Commands, and Army Service Forces, October 7, 1942, decimal file RG 165.
2. Letter from Director Hobby to Truman K. Gibson, Jr., Acting Civilian Aide to the Secretary of War, February 12, 1943, historical file RG 165.

3. AGO 320.2 WAAC PR-WDGAP, Adjutant General's Office to Commanding Generals of Army Service Forces, April 1, 1943, decimal file RG 165.
4. Memorandum from Harriet M. West to Executive through Chief, Operating Service, April 19, 1943, historical file RG 165; Report on Field Trip to Sixth and Seventh Service Commands by Harriet M. West, May 17, 1943, historical file RG 165; SPWA 220.3, Report on Requisitions, June 30, 1943, decimal file RG 165; and SPWA 220.2, Memorandum from the Office of the Director of the WAAC to Howard Clark, Colonel, Director of Operation Division, July 14, 1943, decimal file RG 165. See also SPWA 220.3, Operation Division to Office of Director, July 14, 1943, decimal file RG 165.
5. Letter from H.C. to Colonel Branch, Chief, Planning Service on Motor Transport School (Colored) at Fourth Training Center, April 15, 1943, historical file RG 165; and Letter from Harriet M. West to Executive through Chief, Operating Service, on Progress Report on Motor Transport School Possibilities at Fort Devens, April 19, 1943, historical file RG 165. Evidently, the number of blacks in an activity was the determining factor of whether the activity would be segregated or desegregated. The first OCS classes were segregated, but later classes with fewer blacks were desegregated. Motor Transport School classes at Fort Des Moines were desegregated, but the planning for a Motor Transport School at Fort Devens, which would have a larger number of blacks, called for a segregated activity.
6. Report on Field Trip to Sixth and Seventh Service Commands by Harriet M. West, May 17, 1943, historical file RG 165.
7. Ibid.
8. Memorandum from Harriet M. West to Director, Control Division, May 27, 1943, historical file RG 165.
9. Memorandum from George F. Martin, Major, AUS, Director, Control Division, to Director of WAAC through Executive Office, May 24, 1943, historical file RG 165. Major Martin, apparently in accord with a not uncommon practice among non-blacks, concluded that many blacks were of "inferior" character because of an incident involving a single black woman that occurred at Fort Des Moines shortly before his visit. This incident is discussed in Chapter 5.

10. Ibid.
11. Ibid.
12. SPWA 220.3, Memorandum on requisitions for black units, June 30, 1943, decimal file RG 165.
13. Chart on chronology of WAAC history, n.d., historical file RG 165; SPWA 220.3, Memorandum on requisitions for black units, June 30, 1943, decimal file RG 165; *California Eagle,* December 25, 1942; and *Michigan Chronicle,* December 19, 1942.
14. WAC School Study; *California Eagle,* December 25, 1942; and *Michigan Chronicle,* December 19, 1942. See also SPWA 291.21, Folder on Fort Huachuca, decimal file RG 165.
15. *California Eagle,* December 25, 1942; SPWA 291.21, Folder on Fort Huachuca, decimal file RG 165; and Howard, p. 32.
16. WAC School Study; and newspaper file at Moorland-Spingarn Research Center.
17. *Afro-American* (Washington), March 3, 1945; newspaper file at Moorland-Spingarn Research Center; and Army Directory, June 1945, at Center of Military History, Washington, D.C.
18. WAC School Study; Treadwell, p. 595 and letter from Sylvia Cookman Sellers to author, March 18, 1987.
19. WD WAC 330.14, Report by Harriet M. West, October 27, 1943, decimal file RG 165. On the courts-martials see, for example, General Court-Martial Order No. 133, Army Service Forces, Headquarters. Seventh Service Command, Omaha, Nebraska, February 3, 1944, and General Court-Martial Order No. 152, Army Service Forces, Headquarters, Seventh Service Command, Omaha, Nebraska, February 5, 1944, folders on courts-martial, 250.3 and 291.2, decimal file RG 165.
20. *Chicago Defender,* January 15, 1944; and WAC School Study.
21. 291.2, Memorandum for the Assistant Secretary of War, "Summary Report of Recent Visit of Observation at Southern Camps Relative to Racial Matters," October 3, 1944, decimal file RG 165. This report contains information about some black male units stationed in the South. The memorandum was sent to the assistant secretary of war by the Advisory Committee on Special Troop Policies and among the individuals receiving copies of the summary report were Truman K. Gibson, Jr., and Brigadier General Benjamin O. Davis, Sr.— two blacks—who were probably members of the committee. See also WAC School Study.
22. 291.2, "Summary Report of Recent Visit of Observation at Southern Camps Relative to Racial Matters."

23. Ibid.
24. Ibid.
25. SPWA 220.3, Report of Special Inspection, Camp Brecken-ridge, Kentucky, July 8, 1943, by Don C. Faith, Brigadier General, Director, Inspection Division, decimal file RG 165.
26. 291.2, "Summary Report of Recent Visit of Observation at Southern Camps Relative to Racial Matters"; and SPWA 333.1, Report of Visit to 3564 Service Unit, Colored WAAC Detachment, Fort Knox, by Clara G. H. Man, August 6, 1943, decimal file RG 165.
27. SPWA 333.1, Report of Visit to 3564 Service Unit, Colored WAAC Detachment, Fort Knox.
28. Ibid.
29. 291.2, "Summary Report of Recent Visit of Observation at Southern Camps Relative to Racial Matters."
30. Letter sent to Eleanor Roosevelt, who in turn sent its contents to Colonel Hobby under date of May 4, 1944, without revealing the sender's name, historical file RG 165. Roosevelt felt that the women at Fort Clark were working under a strain and wanted to know if the conditions could be improved. Fort Clark had requisitioned the women to serve as drivers, chauffeurs, hospital orderlies, typists, and clerks (SPWA 220.3, Requisitions for Negro Personnel, June 30, 1943, decimal file RG 165).
31. Letter sent to Eleanor Roosevelt on conditions at Fort Clark; and PLIB 291.2, Church Attendance of Colored Personnel, Headquarters, Army Service Forces, Eighth Service Command, Dallas, Texas, May 4, 1944, historical file RG 165.
32. Field Tour Report, Dorothy L. Meyer to the Director of the WAAC, August 7, 1943, historical file RG 165.
33. Ibid.
34. Ibid. The reporting officer stated that at Fort McClellan blacks were not allowed in the non-commissioned officer club.
35. *Walla Walla Eagle,* August 11, 1943; Album and Scrapbook of Blanche L. Scott, Alexandria, Virginia; and Treadwell, p. 596.
36. September 1943 newspaper clipping in Scott's Album and Scrapbook.
37. Ibid.
38. Treadwell, p. 596.
39. *Salt Tablet,* January 13, 1944; and Scott's Album and Scrapbook.
40. *Sioux City Sunday Journal,* April 2, 1944; and *Bombardier* (Army Air Base, Sioux City), April 8, 1944. These two

newspaper articles may be found in Scott's Album and Scrapbook.

41. *Sioux City Sunday Journal,* April 23, 1944.
42. Ibid.; and Scott's Album and Scrapbook.
43. WD WAC 291.2, Letter from Headquarters, Army Air Force to Jessie Pearl Rice, November 1, 1944, decimal file RG 165; and WD WAC 291.2, Letter from Jessie Pearl Rice to Dorothy C. Stratton, Director, Women's Reserve of United States Coast Guard, November 2, 1944, decimal file RG 165. According to these two letters, among the thirty-five different types of jobs performed by black WACs at army air force installations were automatic equipment mechanic, automatic equipment operator, airplane electrical mechanic, airplane hydraulic mechanic, airplane sheet metal worker, airplane instrument mechanic, airplane engine mechanic, radar repairer, radio mechanic, parachute repairer, parts clerk, motion picture projectionist, administrative specialist, classification specialist, quartermaster supply technician, postal clerk, photographic laboratory technician, mess sergeant, cook, barber, medical administration specialist, and duty non-commissioned officer.
44. SPWA 314.7, Report of WAC Companies, Staff Reports, Elizabeth W. Stearns to Inspector for Director's Office, July 19, 1943, decimal file RG 165.
45. Memorandum from Catherine L. Settle to author, December 22, 1983.
46. Ibid.
47. SPWA 319.1, Letter from Headquarters, Fifth Service Command, Fort Hayes, Columbus, Ohio, to Chief of Staff, June 3, 1943, decimal file RG 165; and SPMDF-10, Memorandum to Surgeon General, Visit to Medical Department Enlisted Technician School and Hospital Detachment, WAC (Colored), Wakeman General Hospital, Camp Atterbury, October 13, 1944, decimal file RG 165.
48. SPMDF-10, Memorandum to Surgeon General, Visit to Medical Department Enlisted Technician School and Hospital Detachment, WAC (Colored), Wakeman General Hospital, Camp Atterbury, October 13, 1944, decimal file RG 165; and WAC School Study.
49. *Toledo Blade,* March 27, 1944; and WAC School Study.
50. WAC School Study.
51. Memorandum for Deputy Director, Bureau of Public Relations, Policy on Recruitment of Negroes for WAC Hospital

Detachment, January 13, 1945, historical file RG 165; and SPDC 291.2, Report of Protest on Assignment of Negro WACs to Gardiner General Hospital, Chicago, Illinois, April 6, 1945, decimal file RG 165. This company was apparently one of the few black hospital units whose personnel received its specialized training at Fort Oglethorpe.

52. SPDC 291.2, Report of Protest on Assignment of Negro WACs to Gardiner General Hospital, April 6, 1945, decimal file RG 165; (CRS) SPJV6 220.3 (WAC), Letter from Russell B. Reynolds to Commanding General, Army Service Forces, April 16, 1945, copy in WAC 291.2, historical file RG 165; 021-031, Hyde Park Community Planning Association, Protests and Responses, under cover letter dated June 25, 1945, General Correspondence of John J. McCloy, Assistant Secretary of War, RG 107; and letters addressed to John J. McCloy from April 1945 to August 1945, subject file RG 107. The groups whose representatives led the protest were the Hyde Park Chamber of Commerce, the Hyde Park Planning Association, the Del Prade Hotel, Glatt and Price Realtors, the Oakland-Kenwood Property Owners, the 53rd Street Business Association, and the 55th Street Business Men's Association.

53. Ibid. For the 1919 race riot in Chicago, see Arthur I. Waskow, *From Race Riot to Sit-in* (New York: Doubleday and Company, Anchor Book, 1967), pp. 38–59.

54. 021-031, Copy of Resolution adopted by Chicago Council Against Racial and Religious Discrimination, General Correspondence of John J. McCloy, subject file RG 107. Copies of this resolution were sent to John J. McCloy, Henry L. Stimson, John R. Hall, the commandant of Gardiner General Hospital, the commanding officer of the black detachment at Gardiner General Hospital, and others.

55. 021-031, Protests and responses under cover letter of John J. McCloy dated June 25, 1945, General Correspondence of John J. McCloy, subject file RG 107; and WAC 320.2, Memorandum, n.d., decimal file RG 165. Letters criticizing the intolerance of the protesting groups and letters congratulating the army for its decision to activate the detachment may be found in 021-031, Protests and responses, General Correspondence of John J. McCloy, subject file RG 107.

56. WAC School Study; Treadwell, pp. 346, 598; Notes from journal of Lieutenant Settle; Letter from Mayor Edward J. Kelly to members of the 55th WAC Hospital Company,

August 14, 1945; and Letter from Westray Battle Boyce, Colonel, GSC, Director, WAC, to Lieutenant Settle, September 1, 1945. Copies of Mayor Kelly's letter and Colonel Boyce's letter are in the possession of the author.

57. Letter from Sylvia Sellers to author, March 18, 1987; telephone interview with Rosine Vance, April 1, 1983; and telephone interview with Liniev Cryer Jones, November 19, 1987.

58. Treadwell, p. 598.

59. Special Orders 203, par. 20, First WAAC Training Center, August 25, 1943; Special Orders 207, par. 25, First WAAC Training Center, August 30, 1943; and interview with Ethel Heywood Smith, February 6, 1990, Silver Spring, Maryland. The company officers were Ethel E. Heywood of Washington, D.C., the commanding officer; Thelma B. Brown of Quitman, Georgia, executive officer; and Julia H. Williams of Birmingham, Alabama, mess and supply officer. Margaret E. Charity of Richmond, Virginia, was the first sergeant (see list of commissioned officers in index and interview with Ethel Heywood Smith, February 6, 1990).

60. Interview with Ethel Heywood Smith, February 6, 1990.

61. Ibid.

62. Special Orders 263, par. 1, November 3, 1943, Army Service Forces, Headquarters, Fourth Service Command; Scrapbook and Album of Ethel Heywood Smith; and Roster of WAC Detachment Number 2, December 25, 1944.

63. WAC School Study; and papers in Bethune Archives.

64. 291.2, Memorandum from William M. Hastie to Director of the WAAC, August 17, 1942, decimal file RG 165; His. 330.14, Official History, WAC, historical file RG 165; Treadwell, pp. 597, 599; SPWA 320.2, CGETO US for London, England, from Marshall to Devers, June 10, 1943, decimal file RG 165 (this communication mentions General Devers's request dated April 10, 1943); and SPWA 320.2, US for London to WAR, June 17, 1943, decimal file RG 165. For black leaders' interest in sending WACs overseas, see SPWA 291.2, Folder on NAACP, decimal file RG 165; WD WAC 330.14, Letter from Jessie Pearl Rice to Bethune, August 16, 1944, decimal file RG 165; papers in the Bethune Archives; and newspaper file at Moorland-Spingarn Research Center.

65. 291.2, "Summary Report of Recent Visit of Observation at Southern Camps Relative to Racial Matters," decimal file RG 165. See also Treadwell, p. 599.

66. Treadwell. p. 599; WA 330.13, Headquarters, 3375th Service Unit, Army Administration School, to Director Hobby, September 10, 1943, decimal file RG 165; and 291.2, Memorandum from Jonathan Daniels to John J. McCloy, December 14, 1944, subject file RG 107.

67. 291.2 Memorandum from Jonathan Daniels to John J. McCloy, December 14, 1944, subject file RG 107; and telephone conversation between Colonel Hobby and General Styler, November 30, 1944, historical file RG 165. The problem was the European Theater of Operation's indecision on the number of women to be sent and the theater's desire to have the unit carried on its table of organization as "overstrength" or overhead.

68. Treadwell, p. 599. Program of welcoming ceremony in Scott's Album and Scrapbook.

69. "A Brief History of the 6888th Central Postal Directory Unit" and "6888th Central Postal Battalion" (copies of these two papers may be found at the Center of Military History, Department of the Army, Washington, D.C.). See also WAC School Study. Bethune had planned to be with Colonel Hobby to bid bon voyage to the women departing for overseas duty. Unable to do so, she sent a telegram, which read: "D.C. 12:43P 2 February 1945 WAC Attn Col Oveta Hobby Camp Shanks NY It was my hope to meet you and confer with you and give my blessings before your departure It is now too late We are depending upon you We have much at stake You represent 15 million of us Your success in this courageous service is ours Think well Realize your individual responsibility Carve a nitch for those who will follow you God bless you Mary McLoud [sic] Bethune National Council of Negro Women" (copy of telegram may be found in the files of Bertie M. Edwards, Tacoma, Washington). On January 15, 1945, when women in the unit were undergoing overseas training at Fort Oglethorpe, the War Department issued a press release announcing the formation of the black unit and stating that it would be sent overseas under the command of black WAC officers (WD, Bureau of Public Relations, Press Branch, Office of Assistant Secretary of War, January 15, 1945, subject file RG 107).

70. *Washington Post,* May 28, 1945. The 6888th did not leave England until May 21, 1945.

71. Memorandum on "Performance of the 6888th Central Postal Directory: The Enlisted Woman's Perspective," from Margaret Young Jackson to author, August 26, 1986. For other accounts

of the unit, see, for example, Tanya L. Demi, "Black Postal Unit," *McClellan News,* February 13, 1985, pp. 14–16; and *Michigan Chronicle,* January 1, 1983. "Tony Brown's Journal" on January 9, 1983, over PBS station WTVS produced a mini-documentary on the 6888th.

72. Memorandum from Margaret Young Jackson to author, August 26, 1986.

73. Ibid.

74. Ibid.

75. Ibid.

76. Ibid.

77. Ibid.

78. Ibid.

79. Letter from Noel C. Mitchell to author, May 12, 1987.

80. His. 314.7, Official Hist., WAC, historical file RG 165; Demi, p. 15; and Treadwell, p. 600.

81. Treadwell, p. 600; Demi, p. 16; and "A Brief History of the 6888th Central Postal Directory Unit."

82. Howard, p. 28; and WAC Necrology—1942–1963, prepared by United States Women's Army Corps School, Fort McClellan, Alabama.

83. WAC School Study; Special Orders No. 376, December 27, 1945, Fourth Service Command, Fort Bragg, North Carolina; and "A Brief History of the 6888th Central Postal Directory Unit."

84. Tanya L. Demi, "Black Female Postal Unit," *McClellan News,* February 13, 1985; and Ethel Payne, "Black Women in the Military: A History of Service," *Delta Journal,* Winter 1986–87, p. 10.

85. From an excerpt of an article in the *Atlanta Journal,* October 5, 1988.

86. Undated clipping from the *Birmingham* (England) *Sunday Mercury,* which may be found in Scott's Album and Scrapbook.

87. Ibid.

88. Ibid.

89. "6888th Central Postal Directory Battalion"; 220.3, Letter from Colonel Westray Boyce to General Paul on return of colored WAC Postal Battalion from ETO, March 21, 1946, decimal file RG 165; and Letter from Colonel Boyce to Assistant Chief of Staff, G-1, on return of colored WAC Postal Battalion from ETO, April 9, 1946, decimal file RG 165. In her March 21, 1946, communication, Boyce complained that she had been expecting a cable from ETO requesting authority to

return all black WAC personnel regardless of whether personnel were eligible for discharge, since the individuals in the unit
were surplus to the needs of the theater. She stated that the
request was never received. Then, she said, she noted a War
Department press release on the arrival of the unit at Camp
Kilmer. The April 9, 1945, communication indicated that the
undesirable conditions under which the black unit was shipped
from the ETO were being investigated.

90. WDGAP 220, To Commanding General, USFET, Main Frank-
furt [*sic*], Germany, December 10, 1945, decimal file RG 165;
220.3-321 WAC, On return to the states of 6888th CPD
during January, December 17, 1945, decimal file RG 165;
220.3-321 WAC, Cable, Return to U.S. all personnel of 6888
CPD during January, December 24, 1945, decimal file RG
165; and 220.3 WAC 321, From Commanding General,
USFET, to War Department, December 28, 1945, decimal file
RG 165.

91. A Department of Defense brochure issued by the Office of the
Deputy Assistant Secretary of Defense for Equal Opportunity
and Safety Policy entitled "Black Americans in Defense of Our
Nation" characterized the inspectors' reports of the unit's
efficiency ratings of less than satisfactory as "inaccurate" and an
"unfair evaluation" (p. 101).

92. *Cleveland Call and Post,* July 20, 1946; *Chicago Defender,*
August 17, 1946; and Treadwell, p. 777. Reentry into the
WAC was authorized by cable on February 9, 1946, but it was
not until August 1946 that the re-entry program was opened to
blacks (WD WAC 342, February 9, 1946, decimal file RG 165;
and WD WAC 342, August 1946, decimal file RG 165).

Chapter 5

1. According to the data compiled by the corps, as of March 31,
1943, about one-third of the 3,000 blacks were high school
graduates and 9 percent were college graduates, compared to
42 percent and 8 percent, respectively, for non-blacks. Among
the blacks, most were twenty-two years old. As of December
31, 1945, the average age of all of the enlisted women in the
corps was twenty-seven, while that of all of the officers was
thirty-two. As of June 30, 1945, 26 percent of the enlisted
women were married, while for the corps as a whole the figure
stood at 10 percent as of March 31, 1946. Questionnaires

completed by twenty-five officers in the 6888th Central Postal Battalion show that seventeen were single, five were married, one was divorced, and two did not respond to this item. These officers' average age was 30.8 years; the oldest was 45 and the youngest was 24. At the time of their entry in the service, three of the officers were students and the rest were gainfully employed. Among 685 enlisted women of the 6888th, although more claimed residence in New York than in any other single state, more than 475 of them claimed residence in states with legalized segregation (Statistical History of the WAAC, June 1943, historical file RG 165; SPKTD WD WAC 353, Memorandum, July 1, 1944, decimal file RG 165; WAC 337, Report to Conference of WAC Staff Directors and Senior Officers, July 11–12, 1946, decimal file RG 165; Official Biographical Record, Public Relations Office, 6888th; and List showing addresses of enlisted women in 6888th [copies of last two documents in possession of author]).

2. Official Biographical Record of 6888th; WD WAC 201, Negro Applicants for first OCS class, decimal file RG 165; newspaper file at Moorland-Spingarn Research Center; and statements in souvenir journals of the five black WAAC/WAC and women in the service reunions.

3. In December 1942, the assistant chief of staff for personnel was informed that the WAAC would provide basic training and certain special training for enlisted women as facilities permitted, and he was also told that when other occupational training was necessary the using service would provide it (SPWA 320.2, Memorandum for Assistant Chief of Staff, G-1, On Recruiting WAC Personnel, December 11, 1942, decimal file RG 165). On advertising for recruiting, see folders SPWA 000.7 and WAAC WD WAC 000.7 decimal file RG 165.

4. Treadwell, p. 59.

5. Excerpt from Stimson's Diary quoted in McGuire, pp. 148–49.

6. Treadwell, p. 594.

7. Ibid., pp. 593–94.

8. Press release, January 9, 1943, historical file RG 165; Memorandum from Harriet M. West to Executive through Chief Operating Service, April 19, 1943, historical file RG 165; and *Afro-American* (Baltimore), November 28, 1942.

9. Letter from Chaplain to Truman K. Gibson, Jr., August 9, 1943, Office of Secretary of War, Civilian Aide to the Secretary, subject file RG 107; Memorandum from Catherine

L. Settle to author, December 22, 1983; and *Chicago Defender*, July 21, 1945.

10. Treadwell, p. 600.

11. *Afro-American* (Washington), March 10, 1945; and Fifth Reunion Souvenir Journal.

12. Report of Trip to Fort Des Moines, n.d., historical file RG 165; Letter from Charity E. Earley to author, August 16, 1987; and 291.2, "Summary Report of Recent Visit of Observation at Southern Camps Relative to Racial Matters," October 3, 1944, decimal file RG 165.

13. *Norfolk Journal and Guide*, April 17, 1943; newspaper file at Moorland-Spingarn Research Center; Roster of 9951st, TSU, SGO, WAC Detachment, Fort Custer, Michigan; Roster of WAC Detachment No. 2, ASF Regional Hospital, Fort Jackson, South Carolina; and Second Reunion Souvenir Journal. The rosters of the two units cited are in possession of the author, as well as a roster containing the names of 709 women, including 24 officers, of the 6888th battalion.

14. STM-30 WD 320.2 OM-S, Strength of the Army, July 1, 1945, p. 71; August 1, 1945, p. 71; and September 1, 1945, p. 72; Center of Military History, Washington, D.C. The Military Personnel Records, Army Reference Branch at the National Personnel Records Center in St. Louis, Missouri, stated that rosters and payrolls for 1944 through 1946 were destroyed in accordance with the general records schedule (Letters from National Records Center, Military Personnel Records, to author, December 7, 1987, and March 4, 1988). The monthly "Strength of the Army" reports contained notices to the numbered recipients to report any errors or discrepancies in the data of their respective units. Hence, the data for any one month was not the final accounting. Compare the figure cited for June 1945 in the "Strength of the Army" report for the total enrollment of the corps with the figure in Appendix 2 for the same month.

15. Roster of WAC Detachment No. 2, Fort Jackson, South Carolina, December 25, 1944; Roster of 9951st Technical Service Unit, Surgeon General's Office, Fort Custer, Michigan; SO 89, Headquarters, United Kingdom Base, APO 413, March 30, 1945, authorized by Headquarters, European TO, March 4, 1945, file AG 322 OpGA, par. 28; and Letter from Sylvia Cookman Sellers to author, March 18, 1987. The special order containing the names of the 685 women of the 6888th

indicated that they were being relieved from an attached unassigned status at the Base Post Office and transferred in grade to the 6888th Central Postal Directory and that the change was organizational in nature with no travel involved. The special order also noted that the 6888th Central Postal Battalion was non–table of organization. A copy of this special order is in possession of the author.

16. Roster of WAC Detachment No. 2, Fort Jackson; Roster 9951st, TSU, Fort Custer; and SO 89, Headquarters United Kingdom Base. The authorized table of organization for WAC companies at army general hospitals was one first sergeant, two technical sergeants, three staff sergeants, three technicians third class, five sergeants, sixteen technicians fourth class, three corporals, sixty-seven technicians fifth class, and two commissioned officers—one a captain and the other a lieutenant. This table of organization was based on units consisting of 100 enlisted women. Although authorized separately, the grades allotted for these companies could be "absorbed . . . with the units assigned to the hospital" (SPAP 341 WAC, Plan for Organization of WAAC Companies in General Hospitals, February 26, 1943, historical file RG 165; and AGPR-1, 341 WAC, Memorandum, n.d. [January 1945], historical file RG 165).

17. Treadwell, p. 775; and newspaper clipping dated May 1, 1945, in Bethune Archives. See also WD WAC 702 folder on pregnancy and separation in decimal file RG 165.

18. SPWA 319.1, Letter from Frank U. McCoskrie to Colonel T. B. Catron, May 13, 1943, decimal file RG 165. WAC policy required the discharge of individuals on certification of pregnancy. If needed, the women could have received assistance from the military personal affairs officer or the American Red Cross. Further, if the women were confined in an army hospital, the confinement would have been at no expense except for subsistence; this benefit was the same as authorized for dependents of enlisted men (WD WAC 702, Letter from Jessie Pearl Rice to Captain Vera E. Von Stern, November 2, 1944, decimal file RG 165).

19. WD WAC 201, Negro Applicants for first OCS class; Official Biographical Record of twenty-five officers of 6888th; WAC School Study; and Norfolk Journal and Guide, March 13, 1943.

20. Ibid.; newspaper file at Moorland-Spingarn Research Center; and scattered documents in RG 165.

21. Official Biographical Record of twenty-five officers of 6888th;

Press release, January 9, 1943, historical file RG 165; WAC School Study; and newspaper file at Moorland-Spingarn Research Center. Not until 1963 did a black WAC officer take the Associate Course at the Command and General Staff School (WAC School Study).

22. SPWA 210.31, OB-S-A-M, January 10, 1943, decimal file RG 165.

23. WD WAC 330.14, Letter from Jessie Pearl Rice to Bethune, August 6, 1944, decimal file RG 165; papers in the Bethune Archives; newspaper file at the Moorland-Spingarn Research Center; WAC School Study; Treadwell, p. 596; and Official Biographical Record of officers of 6888th. In late 1944, Bethune requested permission to visit army camps to assess the conditions under which black women worked. The corps and the army knew that Bethune expressed her concerns about the WAC and the army in public. Possibly in an effort to place a damper on her public statements on matters relating to the military, Colonel Hobby was asked whether Bethune could be taken on as a consultant without pay. Hobby's response was "Not in my shop." She added that she had "used her twice, but I just don't know what she'd do." Hobby then suggested that Bethune be placed in "Truman Gibson's shop" as a consultant. Gibson was the black civilian aide to the secretary of war. Although this suggestion was regarded as a good idea, Bethune's official link to the WAC remained as a member of "General Marshall's Committee," the National Civilian Advisory Committee (telephone conversation between Jonathan Daniels and Hobby, November 29, 1944, historical file RG 165). Harriet M. West's lack of knowledge on the planning for the 6888th and possibly on other matters relating to blacks in the corps was evident from the substance of her conversation with Colonel Rice. In this conversation, West stated that she had obtained information from Truman Gibson, Jr., that "he thought" some blacks were going to be sent overseas and that she understood from Mr. Gibson that "quite a large number will be going" (telephone conversation between Lieutenant Colonel Jessie Pearl Rice and Major Harriet M. West, December 20, 1944, historical file , RG 165).

24. WD WAC 000.7, Letter from Lieutenant Colonel Joseph E. Allen to Colonel J. Noel Macy, Chief, WAC Group, September 14, 1944, decimal file RG 165; and papers in Bethune Archives.

25. WAC School Study; 210.2, Letter from F. U. McCoskrie to

Commanding General, Headquarters, WAC Training Command, October 2, 1943, decimal file RG 165; and Howard, p. 28.

26. Field Tour, Letter from Dorothy L. Meyers to Director of WAC, August 7, 1943, historical file RG 165.

27. For the number of black officers at Fort Des Moines at this time, see 210.2, Letter from F. U. McCoskrie to Commanding General, Headquarters, WAC Training Command, October 2, 1943, decimal file RG 165.

28. SPX 210.2, OB-S-SPGAM, Memorandum on survey of promotion of Negro officers, September 6, 1943, decimal file RG 165. For additional promotions of some of these officers, see undated memorandum in historical file on promotions made in April 1943, August 1943, and September 1943.

29. 210.2, Letter from F. U. McCoskrie to Commanding General, Headquarters, WAC Training Command, October 2, 1943, decimal file RG 165; and 210.31, Letter from Colonel Hobby to Director, Military Personnel, ASF, October 7, 1943, decimal file RG 165. Six months was not the minimum time-in-grade requirement for promotion. As noted, members of the first OCS class received initial promotions after four months. Some of these same officers received second promotions after four months. Some of these same officers received second promotions in April 1943, August 1943, or September 1943. It was not until December 1945, after the war on all fronts had ended, that the War Department sent out a general information memorandum that required that second lieutenants serve six months in-grade for a promotion and that first lieutenants and captains serve twelve months in-grade for promotions (Memorandum, December 11, 1945, historical file RG 165).

30. SPWA 210.31, Policy on Assignment of Negro Officer Personnel, January 10, 1943, decimal file RG 165; 210.2, Policy on Promotion and Assignment of Negro Officer Personnel, January 7, 1944, decimal file RG 165; and 210.2, Letter from Gordon C. Jones to Director of WAC, October 6, 1943, decimal file RG 165. Both the policy on assignment and the policy on promotion and assignment were revisions of previous policy statements.

31. Letter from Walter White, Secretary of NAACP, to Henry L. Stimson, Secretary of War, August 9, 1944, NAACP Papers.

32. WAC School Study shows that eighteen black company commanders were first lieutenants and that two former black company commanders who had been officers since 1943 and

another who was commissioned with the first class were
serving as first lieutenants at the WAC Training Center at Fort
Lee, Virginia, in 1948. Scattered documents in RG 165 reveal
that other black company commanders, some of whom had
been in-grade almost three years, were first lieutenants.

33. Telephone conversation between Colonel Rice and Major
Harriet West, December 20, 1944, historical file RG 165.
Adams had held the rank of major since September 1943,
and she had served in a position that qualified her for a
promotion.

34. Treadwell, p. 597; and telephone conversation between Jonathan Daniels and Colonel Hobby, n.d., historical file RG 165.

35. *Crisis,* July 1918.

36. Memorandum from Mildred C. Kelly to author, April 7, 1986;
and Fifth Reunion Souvenir Journal.

37. Fifth Reunion Souvenir Journal; Third Reunion Souvenir
Journal; and First Reunion Souvenir Journal.

38. Fourth Reunion Souvenir Journal and Second Reunion Souvenir Journal.

39. WAC School Study.

40. Ibid.

41. Ibid.; *Philadelphia Tribune,* April 22, 1947; and newspaper file
at Moorland-Spingarn Research Center.

42. Letter from Margaret Y. Jackson to author, March 19, 1987;
Fifth Reunion Souvenir Journal; First Reunion Souvenir Journal; Second Reunion Souvenir Journal; and SO 89, United
Kingdom Base, APO 413, March 30, 1945, par. 28.

43. Fifth Reunion Souvenir Journal; Second Reunion Souvenir
Journal; and Letter from Margaret Y. Jackson to author, March
19, 1987. Jackson attributed the source of the information on
some of these women to Mattie L. Edmond.

44. Fourth Reunion Souvenir; and notation in memorial program,
January 24, 1987. Copy of memorial program in possession of
author.

45. WAC School Study; Press release, January 9, 1943, historical
file RG 165; papers in Bethune Archives; and Fourth Reunion
Souvenir Journal.

46. Papers in Bethune Archives; WAC School Study; Letter from
Charity E. Earley to author, March 29, 1987; Résumé of
Charity Edna Adams Earley on file at Center of Military
History; Interviews with Dovey J. Roundtree, May 4, 1985;
October 31, 1987; and November 7, 1987; and Fifth Reunion
Souvenir Journal.

Chapter 6

1. 320.2 WAC, Folder on planning for WAC in RA, ORC, and ERC, contains papers dating from January 1, 1946, to December 31, 1946, decimal file RG 165; and Treadwell, pp. 739–43.
2. Treadwell, pp. 746–49.
3. Letter from Charles H. Houston to Walter White, November 3, 1947, and letter from Walter White to Bethune, November 5, 1947, NAACP Papers, Manuscript Division, Library of Congress, Washington, D.C.
4. Franklin, pp. 450–51 and MacGregor, *Integration*, pp. 152–53, 182–89, and 291–312.
5. MacGregor and Natly, *Documents*, 7: 393–402 and 11: 1328–53; and MacGregor, *Integration*, pp. 390–93 and 479–83.
6. WAC School Study; and Women's Army Corps Foundation, *A Date with Destiny*, Fort McClellan, Alabama, 1984).
7. Treadwell, pp. 743–46; WAC School Study; and Reunion Souvenir Journals.
8. WAC School Study; and letter from Alma O. Berry to NAACP, NAACP Papers.
9. AGST-T, letter from A. G. Evans to Commanding General, Fifth Army, December 21, 1951, decimal file RG 165; AGST 210 453WA, letter from Adjutant General to Commanding General of First Army, Attn: Chief, Military Personnel Procurement, January 22, 1952, decimal file RG 165; AGST-O-341 WAC, J. C. Chandler to Chief, Personnel Bureau, November 13, 1952, decimal file RG 165; AG 210.1 WAC, Program for procurement for WAC, Army Reserve Officers at Colleges and Universities, March 20, 1953, and August 5, 1953, decimal file RG 165; AG 421 WAC, DA Cir 32, Section 1, April 24, 1953, decimal file RG 165; AG 421 WAC, letter from Richard S. Whitcomb to Adjutant General, July 3, 1953, decimal file RG 165; AG 342 WAC, letter from Karl A. Zipf to Chief of Publicity Br., January 11, 1954, decimal file RG 165; AGO-WAC 320, letter from Office of Director of WAC to Military Personnel Management Division and Procurement and Distribution Division, and Manpower Control Division, June 6, 1954, decimal file RG 165; and WAC Foundation, *A Date with Destiny*.
10. CSGPA 291.2 WAC, Memorandum from the Director of Personnel and Administration to TAG, on Activation of Negro WAC Detachment in European Command, July 5, 1949, decimal file RG 165.

11. "Strength of the Army" reports.
12. Ibid.
13. Howard, pp. 31–32.
14. Letter from Bernice H. Greene to author, February 27, 1989.
15. Memorandum from Mildred C. Kelly to author, April 7, 1986.
16. Letter from Eunice M. Wright to author, March 3, 1989.
17. Interview with Blanche L. Scott, February 22, 1989; and Scott's Album and Scrapbook.
18. Fifth Reunion Souvenir Journal; WAC School Study; Howard, pp. 31–32; letter from Bernice H. Greene to author, February 27, 1989; and memorandum from Mildred C. Kelly to author, April 7, 1986.
19. WAC School Study; and letter from Eunice M. Wright to author, March 3, 1989.
20. Howard, p. 31; memorandum from Mildred C. Kelly to author, April 7, 1986; and letter from Eunice M. Wright to author, March 3, 1989.
21. Bernard C. Nalty, *Strength for a Fight* (New York: Free Press, 1986), p. 21; Howard, p. 30; memorandum from Mildred C. Kelly to author, April 7, 1986; and MacGregor, *Integration*, pp. 442–49.
22. Memorandum from Mildred C. Kelly to author, April 7, 1986; and letter from Bernice H. Greene to author, February 27, 1989.
23. Letter from Eunice M. Wright to author, March 3, 1989.
24. *Washington Post*, February 18, 1989, and March 1, 1989.

BIBLIOGRAPHY

Manuscripts

Atlanta, Army Service Forces, Headquarters, Fourth Service Command. Special Orders 263, par. 1, November 3, 1943.

Fort Bragg, North Carolina. Fourth Service Command. Special Order No. 376, December 27, 1945.

Fort Custer, Michigan. Surgeon General's Office. Roster of 6651st Technical Service Unit.

Fort Des Moines, Iowa. First Women's Army Auxiliary Corps Training Center. Unnumbered Memorandum, August 23, 1943.

———. Unnumbered Memorandum, September 4, 1943.

———. Special Orders 203, par. 20, August 25, 1943.

———. Special Orders 207, par. 25, August 30, 1943.

Fort Jackson, South Carolina. Army Service Forces Regional Hospital. Roster of WAC Detachment No. 2, December 25, 1944.

Fort McClellan, Alabama. Women's Army Corps School. WAC Necrology—1942–1963, 1963.

Fort Oglethorpe, Georgia. Third Women's Army Corps Training Center. Special Order No. 268, paragraphs 1 and 3, October 16, 1943.

United Kingdom, Base APO 413. Special Order No. 89, paragraphs 27 and 28, March 30, 1945.

———. Public Relations Office. 6888th Central Postal Battalion. Official Biographical Records of Officers.

———. Roster Showing Addresses of Enlisted Women.

Washington, D.C. Bethune Archives. Papers on the Women's Army Corps.

———. Department of the Army. United States Army Judiciary. CM 274866.

———. Library of Congress. Manuscript Division. Papers of the National Association for the Advancement of Colored People.

———. United States War Department. Adjutant General's Office. AGPO-S-201, Pace, December 13, 1945.

———. United States War Department. Center of Military History. Army Directory: Continental United States Monthly Reports, 1943 to 1946.

———. United States War Department. Center of Military History. Strength of the Army Monthly Reports, 1942 to 1978.

———. United States War Department. National Archives. General Correspondence of John J. McCloy. Office of the Secretary of War, Assistant Secretary of War. Record Group 107.

———. United States War Department. National Archives. Army G-1, WAAC/WAC Decimal File Record Group 165.

———. United States War Department. National Archives. Army G-1, WAAC/WAC Historical Background File Record Group 165.

———. United States War Department. National Archives. Office of Assistant Secretary of War, Civilian Aide to the Secretary. Record Group 107.

Newspapers

Afro-American (Baltimore), September 5, 1942; November 21, 1942; and March 10, 1945.

——— (Richmond), February 13, 1943.

——— (Washington, D.C.), July 10, 1943; March 3, 1945; and March 10, 1945.

Amsterdam Star News, August 12, 1944; and July 28, 1945.

Atlanta Journal, October 5, 1988.

Birmingham World, July 24, 1942.

Bombardier (Army Air Base, Sioux City, Iowa), April 8, 1944.

California Eagle, December 25, 1942.

Chicago Defender, September 5, 1942; November 2, 1942; February 27, 1943; September 4, 1943; January 15, 1944; July 21, 1945; and August 17, 1946.

Cleveland Call and Post, July 20, 1946.

Des Moines Register, September 12, 1943; and September 22, 1943.

Detroit Tribune, August 29, 1942.

Houston Informer, May 26, 1944.

Louisville (Kentucky) *Defender,* February 27, 1943.

Michigan Chronicle, December 19, 1942; and January 1, 1983.

New York Age, January 9, 1943; and August 18, 1945.

Newspaper File on Black Women in the Military, Moorland-Spingarn Research Center, Howard University, Washington, D.C.

Norfolk Journal and Guide, November 21, 1942; March 13, 1943; April 17, 1943; and April 21, 1945.

Oklahoma Eagle, February 1945.

Philadelphia Tribune, September 5, 1942; October 12, 1942; October 19, 1942; November 7, 1942; January 9, 1943; and April 22, 1947.

Pittsburgh Courier, April 28, 1945.

P.M., March 21, 1945.

Portsmouth Star, April 11, 1943.

Salt Tablet, January 13, 1944.

Sioux City Sunday Journal, April 2, 1944; and April 23, 1944.

Toledo (Ohio) *Blade*, March 27, 1944.

Walla Walla Eagle, August 11, 1943.

Washington Post, June 30, 1943; March 21, 1954; March 23, 1945; April 28, 1945; May 28, 1985; February 18, 1989; and March 1, 1989.

Washington Star, November 19, 1942.

Correspondence

Bethune, Mary McLeod, to Colonel Oveta Hobby. February 2, 1945. Copy in author's possession.

Boyce, Westray Battle, Colonel, General Staff Corps, Director, WAC, to Lieutenant Settle. September 1, 1945. Copy in author's possession.

Earley, Charity E., to author. March 29, 1987, and August 16, 1987.

Edwards, Bertie M., to author. June 15, 1988.

Greene, Bernice H., to author. February 27, 1989.

Jackson, Margaret Y. Performance of the 6888th Central Postal Directory: The Enlisted Women's Perspective. To author. August 26, 1986.

———. To author. March 19, 1987.

Kelly, Edward J., Mayor of Chicago. To members of 55th WAC Hospital Company. August 14, 1945. Copy in author's possession.

Kelly, Mildred C., to author. April 17, 1986.

Mitchell, Noel C., to author. May 12, 1987.

Sellers, Sylvia C., to author. March 18, 1987.

Settle, Catherine L., to author. December 22, 1983, and December 28, 1983.

Wright, Eunice M., to author. February, 1989.

Interviews

Campbell, Vera G. New York, New York. Undated [1949].

Jones, Liniev C. Washington, D.C., January 20, 1987, and November 19, 1987. Telephone interviews.

McRae, Ina. New York, New York. Undated.

Roundtree, Dovey M. Washington, D.C., April 27, 1985; May 4, 1985; October 31, 1987; and November 7, 1987.

Scott, Blanche L. Washington, D.C., and Alexandria, Virginia. April 4, 1988, and February 22, 1989.

Simmons, Juliette. Washington, D.C. May 22, 1988. Telephone interview.

Smith, Ethel Heywood. Washington, D.C., and Silver Spring, Maryland. May 22, 1988; May 25, 1988; June 6, 1988; February 6, 1990.

Vance, Rosine. Washington, D.C. April 1, 1983. Telephone interview.

Books, Articles, Reports, and Journals

A Brief History of the 6888th Central Postal Directory Unit. Center of Military History. Washington, D.C.

Crisis, July 1918.

Demi, Tanya L. "Black Postal Unit." *McClellan News,* February 13, 1985, pp. 14–16.

Franklin, John Hope. *From Slavery to Freedom: A History of Negro Americans.* 5th ed. New York: Alfred A. Knopf. 1980.

Howard, Grendel. "Carrying Forth a Tradition." *Soldiers,* February 1985, pp. 28–32.

Lee, Ulysses. *The Employment of Negro Troops.* Washington, D.C.: Government Printing Office. 1966.

MacGregor, Morris J., Jr. *Integration of the Armed Forces, 1940–1965.* Washington, D.C.: Government Printing Office. 1981.

MacGregor, Morris J., Jr., and Nalty, Bernard C., eds. *Blacks in the United States Armed Forces: Basic Documents.* Vol. 5. Wilmington: Scholarly Resources, 1977.

Macy, J. Noel. "Negro Women in the WAC." *Opportunity* 23 (Winter 1945): 14.

McGuire, Philip. "Desegregation in the Armed Forces: Black Leadership, Protest and World War II." *Journal of Negro History* 68 (Spring 1983): 174–258.

Memorial Program for Rosine Vance, January 22, 1987. Washington, D.C.

Nalty, Bernard C. *Strength for a Fight.* New York: Free Press. 1986.

Payne, Ethel. "Black Women in the Military: A History of Service." *Delta Journal,* Winter 1986/87, pp. 7–10.

Redd, Lavinia L. History of Military Training, WAAC/WAC Training. Center of Military History. Washington, D.C.

Résumé of Charity Edna Adams. Center of Military History. Washington, D.C.

Reunion Journals:
    First Negro WAAC/WAC Reunion Journal. Dallas, Texas. October 13–16, 1978.

Second Reunion of Black Military Women of World War II. Los Angeles, California. October 16–19, 1980.
Third WAC Reunion. Detroit, Michigan. August 19–22, 1982.
Fourth Black Women's Army Auxiliary Corps and Women's Army Corps Reunion. Atlanta, Georgia. October 3–7, 1984.
Black WAAC/WAC and Women in the Service Reunion (Fifth). Washington, D.C. October 2–5, 1986.

Scott, Blanche L. Album and Scrapbook. Alexandria, Virginia.

Settle, Martha A. Journal. Washington, D.C.

Smith, Ethel Heywood. Album and Scrapbook. Bethune Archives. Washington, D.C.

Treadwell, Mattie E. *Women's Army Corps*. Washington, D.C.: Government Printing Office. 1954.

United States. Department of Defense. Office of the Deputy Assistant Secretary of Defense for Equal Opportunity and Safety Policy. "Black Americans in Defense of Our Nation." 1985.

————. Report of the President's Committee on Civil Rights. "To Secure These Rights." 1947.

————. Women's Army Corps. Division of Doctrine and Literature. "Summary of Information on Negro Women Who Have Served or Are Serving in the Women's Army Corps, 1942–1963." Fort McClellan Alabama. 1963.

————. War Department. *A Manual for Courts-Martial, U.S. Army*. Washington, D.C.: Government Printing Office. 1928; corrected to April 20, 1943.

Waskow, Arthur. *From Race Riot to Sit-in*. New York: Doubleday and Company, Anchor Book. 1967.

Women's Army Corps Foundation. *A Date with Destiny*. Fort McClellan, Alabama. 1984.

ABOUT THE AUTHOR

MARTHA S. PUTNEY (A.B. and M.A., Howard University; Ph.D., University of Pennsylvania) is a retired Professor of History. She was a Danforth Foundation Fellow in Black Studies and has taught at Morgan State College, Bowie State College, and Howard University. Dr. Putney presently serves on the editorial board of the *Journal of the Afro-American Historical and Genealogical Society*. She has read papers at annual meetings of professional societies and has had more than fifteen articles published in professional journals. Her *Black Sailors: Afro-American Merchant Seamen and Whalemen Prior to the Civil War* (Greenwood Press) was published in 1987. She has served as a commissioned officer in the Women's Army Corps.

CPSIA information can be obtained at www.ICGtesting.com
Printed in the USA
LVOW11s1536301214

420938LV00002B/301/P

1/28/15